Penguin Books
Daughters of Rachel

Natalie Rein was born in London, into a family
with an immigrant Jewish background. She
studied Social Administration at the London
School of Economics and now works in management
in a Social Services Department of a London
Borough Local Authority.

It was during the years that she, her husband and
their three daughters lived in Israel that Natalie
Rein became active in the Women's Movement.
Since returning to England, she has visited Israel
on several occasions to research this book and
to keep in contact with many activists of the
Women's Movement there.

ASC

Natalie Rein

DAUGHTERS OF RACHEL

Women in Israel

Penguin Books

Penguin Books Ltd, Harmondsworth,
Middlesex, England
Penguin Books, 625 Madison Avenue,
New York, New York 10022, U.S.A.
Penguin Books Australia Ltd, Ringwood,
Victoria, Australia
Penguin Books Canada Limited, 2801 John Street,
Markham, Ontario, Canada L3R 1B4
Penguin Books (N.Z.) Ltd, 182–190 Wairau Road,
Auckland 10, New Zealand

First published in Pelican Books in Great Britain 1980
First published in Penguin Books in the United States of America 1980

Printed in the United States of America by
Offset Paperback Mfrs., Inc., Dallas, Pennsylvania
Set in Linotype Juliana

Contents

TO MY SISTER OLGA

Introduction

Because of the nature of this book, its subject matter and its geographical base, it is necessary at the outset to give an account of myself and to offer my credentials as its author. Not, of course, an account of my domestic and personal life – a set of gossipy details carefully watered-down and made respectable for my readership. What I must do is show how, not having been born an Israeli, I feel I have a right to identify with the country and its people and to write about them. Much of what will come later will help to create an ambiguity in my position, but since my position is symbolic of the essence of the problems involved, that ambiguity is essential to the authenticity of the work.

To say I have a right to express myself on this subject because I am a descendant of Eve would be arrogant, superficial and pretentious. We are, all of us, if we subscribe to such a theory, descendents of Eve, as our brothers are descendents of Adam and as such this affords us no privileges. Indeed, had our genesis from that lady been more sympathetically described we might all have felt more able to accept her as our original mother. Much can be attributed to that!

But later than that and from the same source, I can claim a fairly unbroken line from Miriam, sister of Moses and Aaron; Rachel, wife of Jacob; Sarah, the wife of Abraham; the sensitive dutiful Ruth and the brave, powerful Esther. These women moulded me, I suspect. Their names alone were handed down through generations of my ancestors to arrive as identification for my great-grandmothers, grandmothers, aunts, cousins. Their husbands, fathers, nephews, also my kin, were Solomon, Abraham, Isaac, Jacob, Moses, David. And as well as with their names, I grew up with their laws, traditions, customs, rules, myths, standards and values. And so did my sisters in Eastern Europe,

America, France, Morocco, Algeria, South Africa and Israel. In short, I am a Jew and a woman.

But, again, to assume that being a Jew and a woman gives me some claim to being an authority on the subject of feminism in Israel would be to make a false declaration. All Jews would like to claim this right; all Jews think they know more about the heart of Israel than the Israelis themselves and all Jews in the Diaspora would like to control, with their wealth and their emotional black-mail, the behaviour of the Israelis. No! This woman-jew lived in Israel between 1971 and 1973, helped to form the Women's Move-ment and has kept in close touch both with the country and its women ever since. The connection, therefore, with my ancestry and with Israel confirms for me my own identity and joins me, in every sense, to the subject of this book and to the nature of the problems and dilemmas contained therein.

The main thing I learnt even on my first visit to Israel (to be confirmed time and again as my familiarity with the country grew) was the relationship and tie between Israeli Jews and the Jews of the Diaspora. It is a relationship based on an arrogant belief by Jews in the *Golah* that Israelis are the same as they are, that the experiences of the Israelis are the experiences of Am-erican Jews, British Jews, French Jews, South African Jews. The rigid traditionalism of these Jews of the Diaspora does not allow them to see how outside influences and specific national experi-ences have affected and moulded them and, by the same token, how the specific national experiences of the Israelis have moulded them. Because of their narrowness, these Jews of the outside world, many of them Zionists, coming to Israel, do not identify themselves with the Israelis but at once identify the Israelis with themselves. They think there is no problem of cultural assimi-lation for Jews going to Israel. They know there may be problems related to day-to-day living. The Middle East has a special quality they do not expect to understand. But, at a level of consciousness where fundamental, personal decisions are taken; where attitudes, values and emotions are established; where people feel, express what they feel and then act on that expression of feeling; those areas, in fact, where people grow into a nation; that level, according to the World Zionist Movement, must take place in the context of international Jewishness.

I prefer to use the word 'Jewishness' (in Yiddish – the universal language of European, *Ashkenazi* Jews – '*Yiddishkeit*') rather than Judaism because Jewishness is that state of being a Jew through the pores, without needing to refer to an ideology or to abide by any principles. Jewishness is the collective experience of Jews: the flight from Spain in the fifteenth century; the persecutions through the Middle Ages; the Eastern European pogroms and repressions; Hitler. It is abiding by British laws, French laws, South African and American laws but, at the same time, maintaining your Jewishness. On Friday evening, in any town in the West, knock on any door of any house where a *mezuzah* hangs on the jamb and when that door is opened you will find candles lit and the whole paraphernalia of Jewishness. It does not matter if you are in London, Glasgow, Houston, New York, Buenos Aires or Marseilles, all the Jews you meet will have a common understanding of Jewishness. Among other things it is honouring the mother to the extent of creating the 'Jewish Mother' syndrome; it is 'Portnoy's Complaint';[1] it is thousands of years of circumcision, incantation, mumbo-jumbo and superstition but most of all, perhaps, it is the six thousand years of a cultural heritage moulded and cemented by persecution, by being hated, by being despised for being different; by being loathed for its closeness when it was stripped of everything but its closeness to give it strength.

These illustrations are not intended to offer sentimental excuses for a maudlin approach to an important and significant race. They are intended to offer to the reader an understanding of the significance of Jewishness in the context of Israel. For this Jewishness forms a relationship with Israel which needs to be explained and understood, as it is probably the fundamental, controlling, inhibiting element in the fight for female emancipation in that country.

Israel was born out of Zionism and Jewishness. It was the very Jewishness of Jews which incensed Hitler and led to the holocaust. This in turn gave the final push to the creation of the Jewish State in Palestine – a cause which had been in existence long before Hitler and which was based on the principles of Zionism. From the dream of the early pioneers for a Jewish State in Palestine which would establish its own identity in the Middle East, the new State, when it came about in 1948, became instead a haven for the conservation of a culture. The very people who earlier had wanted desperately to reject that culture found themselves building a State to protect it. The remnants of the Jewish population in Europe brought with them their grief, their guilt, and those parts of Judaism and Jewishness they could carry in their souls, parts which, with time, had become idealized and made all the more precious for the suffering. The need to cling to those parts of the past which gave an identity and helped to maintain a sort of equilibrium *in extremis* had a powerful effect on the life of the new State. Instead of the country moving forward at a pace and in a way dictated by local circumstances, ambience and conditions, it remained emotionally at a standstill, gasping for breath.

The life-styles created by the Zionists who had long settled in Palestine and who had fought for their survival were suddenly brought into open confrontation with a culture they had been deliberately trying to deny. And the culture of European Jewry, the culture which had as its elements the whole force of quasi-religious paternalism, traditionalism, bigotry, suspicion, panic and fear, triumphed. The State of Israel returned, in many respects, to the ghetto and it was this image of itself which proved acceptable to World Jewry and which, as a result, continued to reinforce itself within the country. This traditional form of Jewishness quelled the fears of all those Jews of the Diaspora who thought that Zionism would destroy the image of the Jew and would put in its place a new individual with whom they would be expected to identify but could not and on whom they might one day be dependent. This person should have been the 'Am Ha'aretz', the 'man of the soil', free thinking, Godless, hardworking and un-schooled in the claustrophobic, neurotic principles of fundamental Judaism – yet undeniably a Jew.

But as a result of the holocaust, these fears were groundless. The survivors went to Israel on their own terms and in the prevailing chaos, the mêlée, the shock, horror, guilt, those terms and their needs were inevitably respected. The State of Israel became kosher!

Slowly then, the country moved back in the direction of European Jewishness and the acceptance this gained in the eyes of the outside world, especially the United States, became important to the State. The Jews of the United States could identify with a traditional Israel, an Israel which adhered closely to custom, which maintained a respect for its Jewish religious laws, its dietary laws, its laws regarding the Sabbath and which accepted once again the whole basis of conventional Jewish life. As a result, money poured in from America, Britain, South Africa, everywhere in the West where there were Jews. The State, like God, was an insurance, not only for Jews themselves but for Jewishness itself and all that it implied. The continuous reinforcement of this gave Jews a confidence in themselves – a confidence clearly illustrated by the powerful Jewish lobby in the United States, the moderating of overt anti-semitism in Europe and the continuing faith of World Jewry in Israel.

It is because of the power of this Jewishness that I have the confidence to write about an aspect of Israeli life with which I am familiar. All this, then, gives me my base and I have chosen to describe it at this early stage because of its power and importance. As it has influenced me, so it has influenced my sisters in Israel and totally affected their position in the country. The Israeli Women's Movement has been the outcome of this conflict.

In any movement concerned with social and human progress there are many and subtle factors which play their part in turning an idea into a cause. Indeed it is the more subtle factors, the inter-relationships between people and ideas, between ideas and existing values, between fashions and philosophies and between fads and fundamental principles which may create positive forces capable of survival (like Zionism itself – or Fascism). It is at this subliminal level that it is necessary to examine any radical ideology. My emphasis on Jewishness is essential in this context as Israel consists of a majority of Jews (around three million), but there are also other important ethnic groups whose place and position in the country are paramount and whose women are not exempt from oppression and subjection. Among the forces ruling women in Israel, to the all pervading, deferential controlling power of Judaism must be added the severe discipline of Islam, a devout Christianity overlaid with the spirit of the misogynistic Paul, the Druse culture, apart and private, the Greek Orthodox, the Russian Orthodox, the Bahai, all with their special brand of machismo.

This is the society in which the women are trying to find themselves, their identity as women, their sense of self, their charisma. This book is an attempt to analyse their chances.

ACKNOWLEDGEMENTS

Among all the people who have given me help and encouragement while writing this book I would particularly like to thank Geraldine Cooke of Penguin for her patience and the long hours spent with me on many occasions; my husband, Sydney, for his advice, interest, concern and care; Nava Schreiber and Noya Biegeleisen for interminable translations; the Wiener Library in London who spared no effort in their attempts to help me find rare material; and, of course, all my friends in Israel who, whether they were feminists or not, gave me warmth, love and unstinted help.

PART ONE

1. From *Shtetl* to *Yishuv*

When reading the history of the Jews and studying the development of Zionism, it would almost appear as if women did not exist. Seldom, in the vast library of Judaica, are women given pride of place either for heroic acts or deeds, or as making individual contributions to their society, or as a group with special needs, interests or desires. The Old Testament has only two books devoted to women – Ruth and Esther; the former offering us four chapters and the latter, ten. The plight of Jews is discussed in terms of men, the historic role of education of Jews is concerned with men and the continuous and lengthy interpretation and re-interpretation of Jewish laws, customs and traditions is totally male-orientated. Zborowski and Herzog write:

> The good wife and mother helps her husband to fulfil his obligations. She is responsible for the observance of the dietary laws and for maintaining and implementing all the domestic ritual. Even when her husband performs the ceremony it is her duty to have in readiness the cup of wine, the loaf of bread, the knife, the towel, the incense or whatever is needed. She is not included in religious ritual outside the house and, in fact, is not expected to be familiar with it. Moreover, she does not have powers of discretion even in household ceremonials. On any problem of observance she must consult a man – her husband, her rabbi, a respected scholar – and even if she knows the answer herself, by experience, she has not the right to decide for herself.[1]

From the earliest times, and everywhere where Jews have been denied civil rights in the host country, power, influence and decision making have taken place around the synagogue and the elders of the synagogue – an exclusive male society. In the synagogue there is no precedent for the involvement of women who are not even expected to be present at prayer. In fact they are, and have always been, totally excluded from all forms of prayer-making, except that of candle lighting at home on the Sabbath eve. Rabbi Dr Isadore Epstein, a leading authority on Judaism, described the differences:

The obligation of positive commands begins, strictly speaking, on the completion of the thirteenth year when a Jewish boy reached his legal majority, *Bar Mitzvah*. On attaining that age he is confirmed in his duties and privileges by putting on the *tefillin* and being 'called up' to the public reading of the Torah ... Women are exempt from many of the positive commands which must be performed within certain prescribed times. This exemption is not a mark of women's inferiority but is in accordance with the Talmudic principle that 'one who is engaged in one religious act is exempt from claims of another upon him'. The vocation of womanhood is in itself considered of a sufficiently sacred character as to engage a woman's attention to the exclusion of any other religious duties which must be performed at any given time and which consequently might interfere with her special tasks ... The religious majority of girls begins at the age of twelve years and one day, with no particular celebration to mark the occasion as, in the absence of positive commands in their case, confirmation in the Judaic sense of the word is of little relevance.[2]

Jewish religious laws and traditions explicitly deny women the right to participate in order that they may not be distracted from the role of servant, 'home-maker' and general family drudge. And while the synagogue and its form of social control and domination placed serious responsibilities and burdens on the men, it nevertheless gave the tone and status to their lives. And they were totally honoured. The religion demanded obedience, an obedience which, uniquely, ennobled and enriched them. For the women it offered only subservience, obedience and passivity.

It was a woman, although not a Jewish woman, who probably polarized for millions of Jewish women their status of inferiority. That woman was the Empress, Catherine II of Russia (1762–96). While the Jews of Western Europe were being given equal rights and freedom of religious worship within the wider community by the Emperor Napoleon, the largest group of Ashkenazi Jews (around six million) were living under the reign of Catherine the Great and subsequent Tsars. She was not prepared to allow these Jews of Russia and Poland freedom of movement and equal rights but instead contained them within an area known as the Pale of Settlement. This was an area on the outskirts of the large towns of Russia, Poland, Romania and Galicia to which Jewish rights of residence were restricted. The aim of the regulation was to curtail the movement of Jews and to keep them from constituting a threat either to the farming communities living in the countryside or the merchants living in the towns.

The right to live wherever they chose and to travel freely throughout Russia belonged only to Jews with University degrees, as well as to dentists and pharmacists. The privileged category also included pharmacists' assistants, male nurses and midwives, but these enjoyed only a so-called 'conditional right of residence' restricted to the places where they practised their professions ... The right to residence outside the Pale was also granted to certain artisans. However, the residence right was available only to Jewish artisans who were in fact plying their trade in the given place and had a certificate to that effect from the local Trades Board.[3]

Along with this grave curtailment of liberty, Catherine the Great and subsequent Tsars indulged in continuous discriminatory legislation causing greater and greater hardship to the Jews of the Pale.

Matters came to a head after Catherine's death, under the weak régime of Paul I (1796–1801), in 1799. A severe famine ravaged many western districts. To answer the grievances of the suffering farmers the Government decided to consult the assemblies of landlords in Minsk and other provinces ... It may have been well aware that the mismanagement of their estates by those very landlords and the entire institution of serfdom were mainly responsible for these catastrophic shortages ... Understandably these nobles did not blame themselves but rather explained the failures through natural and other causes, aggravated by the Jewish innkeepers' exploitation of the peasants. Their suggestions culminated in ousting Jews from the entire liquor industry and the handing over of all production and distribution thereof directly to the landlords or their appointees.[4]

On the same subject, Louis Greenberg writes. 'The edict ... proved disastrous because the government had made no provision for the absorption of the evicted population into other occupations ... (it) brought ruin upon 60,000 Jewish families – about half a million souls.' He notes, too:

In 1821, Jews were forbidden to come to the interior Russian provinces even for business purposes. In 1825, the provinces of Astrakan and the Caucasus which had been open to Jews since 1804, were declared closed to them. In the same year, the existing population of residence in the province of Vohlyn, within a radius of fifty versts from the border, was extended to all border states. Even Prince Galitsyn, a historian who lauded the Jewish policies of Alexander I testifies to the misery experienced by the Jews during that emperors reign. 'One cannot deny,' he states, 'that during the period Jews were destined to suffer. Jewish tears flowed freely.' Restrictive measures multiplied rapidly in the reign of Nicholas I, pointing to a desire on the part of the Government to cut Jews off from Russian life, rather than to make them a part of it.[5]

The Pale, these little places, neither towns nor villages, in which the large majority of the Jews of Eastern Europe lived, were known by them as the *shtetl*, and it was in the shtetl that they moulded their lives and eked out an existence from the late eighteenth century until the early twentieth century (a period covering about 150 years). It was from the shtetl that many of the early Palestinian settlers originated and it was a reaction to shtetl life which helped to form the philosophy of the early Zionists.

In general, shtetl life was intolerable. The harsh régime of the Romanoffs[6] and their frenzied hatred of Jews caused unbearable hardship. Wave after wave of hooligans attacked the shtetl causing death and misery. These 'pogroms', sanctioned by the ruling classes and ignored by the police, came to be an integral part of life in the shtetl. The Jews of the Pale were deprived of human rights, unable to progress, were forbidden access to the normal life of the country, and remained uneducated, illiterate and ignorant. The historians Frumkin, Aronson and Goldenweiser investigate some of the reasons:

The quota established for Jews in schools within the Pale of Settlement was ten per cent, outside the Pale it was five per cent and in St Petersburg and Moscow, only three per cent. Similar quotas were soon introduced for the admission of Jews to universities and other high educational institutions. Like all the laws concerning the Jews, these regulations were considered 'temporary'. However, they remained in force until the Revolution of 1917.[7]

In the face of violence, rabid anti-semitism and loathing the people of the shtetl grew more and more enclosed, suspicious, fearful and bitter. Louis Golding, in his book *The Jewish Problem*, writes:

The self-defence units which some of the more spirited of the younger generation formed were, of course, condemned as illegal and provocative. In 1903, there took place the bloody massacre at Kishinev, which lasted for three days and sent a wave of horror throughout the world. From 1905 to 1909 alone, it was reckoned that there were 284 outbreaks, and no fewer than 50,000 victims. Meanwhile, the economic condition of the Jews was made impossible by the May Laws[8] which the Government had issued in 1881 (ostensibly as a temporary expedient), on the principle that a minority which is attacked must necessarily require radical remedial treatment ... These outbursts (imitated on a small scale, but more ingeniously, in Roumania) almost broke the spirit of Eastern European Jewry.[9]

In their retreat from the horrors of life under the Tsars, and in order to maintain reality, they withdrew into an isolated world of fanatical religious observance. Religion had always been pre-eminent in Jewish life but now it became the very vehicle of survival itself. Devoid of all possibilities of self-expression, creativity and progress in the outside world, it was for the men both a release of spiritual and emotional feelings together with an escape from the deprivations of life. Irving Howe reflects on this:

The condition of permanent precariousness gave the East European Jews a conscious sense of being at a distance from history as such and history as a conception of the Western world. Living in an almost timeless proximity with the mythical past and the redeeming future, with Abraham's sacrifice of his beloved son to a still more beloved God and the certain appearance of a cleansing Messiah – for heaven was real, not a useful myth, and each passing day brought one nearer to redemption – the Jews could not help feeling that history was a little ridiculous, an often troublesome trifling of the gentile era.[10]

As a result of this deprivation, the main and most hallowed occupation was to study in the synagogue or the *yeshiva* and to follow the Jewish laws and customs to the letter.[11] Even this was only for the privileged. The rest of the community – and this, of course, included all the women – scratched a living as pedlers, small shopkeepers and artisans, and in general people lived in grinding poverty.

Because of the lack of source material it is difficult to build up a picture of the women of the shtetl. Yet these were women who, in spite of everything, upheld the practicalities of life, raised the children, took care of the needs of the men and often brought financial support to the family. Zborowski and Herzog describe them thus:

> The woman's world is outside the kheyder and the besmidresh. For the most part women are barely literate in Yiddish and cannot understand the Hebrew they read ... Since study of the divine Law, the primary status criterion, is not for women, they are automatically excluded from top honours in the community. A woman's formal status is indirect. It relates not to herself as an individual but to her position as wife and mother. For men there is the title 'Reb' but for women there is no corresponding generalised title. She may be referred to as the wife of her husband, 'Isaac's Sara' and addressed by her name without a title, or as 'housewife' (Balebosteh).[12]

For them life and religion meant hardship, deprivation and slavery with no rewards. For the men there was acceptance in the eyes of God; learning, the development of the intellect (even though in a narrow, ecclesiastical environment) for which they were honoured beyond measure and, whenever possible, the chance of advancement in the outside world. The women lived in the deep shadows of their men.

From birth, girls were given no place in the family. They were a burden with no future save that of marriage and children, particularly sons. The single woman had no identity if she was not a wife or a prospective bride. She developed no skills, talents, aspirations which might conflict with this role. Zborowski and Herzog write: 'To be a spinster is a dreadful fate, which fortunately occurs far more in the anxious forebodings of girls and their parents than in fact. The shtetl does not provide a place for an "alteh moyd" (old maid).'[13] Yet, even marriage itself was, for the woman, undignified and humiliating. Her marriage was always arranged by her father and the shtetl marriage-broker and generally she did not meet her husband until the wedding day. The marriage ceremony was preceded by a degrading period of haggling by husband and father over her dowry and the husband's ability to support his wife, which, for reasons aforementioned, he rarely did. She was only marriageable with a dowry. Poor girls and those from families with many daughters had great difficulty in finding husbands. She had no say in choosing whom she was to marry nor when. Since marriage was the only aspiration of Jewish girls and since daughters were considerable burdens on the family they were married off at an early age, often to men many years older than themselves. On marriage, women's heads were shaved and remained so throughout their lives. As a substitute for their own hair married women wore ugly, characterless wigs. Any outward signs of physical attractiveness in women was strictly forbidden so as not to provide temptations for the men. 'A woman is considered so potent a source of attraction that a man must avert his eyes in order to protect them both. Some men will not even speak directly to a woman.' 'Extreme avoidance of women by men is the prescribed pattern of the shtetl.'[14]

Yet, for all this, marriage itself held no hope of growth or development since neither husband nor wife held expectations of unity or closeness. Jewish marriage in the shtetl was not concerned with the merging of souls or the building of close love ties or bonds.

Love, as such, and certainly romantic love, was not considered of primary importance in initiating or even maintaining the union. The paramount objective was to perpetuate and guarantee the survival of the new generation. The mother's task was to protect and nurture the children while serving as a devoted and chaste wife who might eventually become her husband's footstool in heaven.[15]

Zborowski and Herzog also refer to her unfortunate position:

The formal demands upon women are revealed repeatedly in comments on womanly virtue. 'She was a perfect Jewish woman, clean, patient, hard-working and silent, submissive to God and to her husband, devoted to her children ... her own wellbeing was unimportant ... I don't remember my mother sitting at the table when we ate, except on Friday and Saturday night.'[16]

Sons, on the other hand, were sanctified from birth. From an early age they were taught to understand the world of scholarship through the synagogue, learning the language of the prayers and understanding all its manifestations, so that they could, in their turn, achieve a state of honour and respect in the community. Zborowski and Herzog were quite clear on the effect of this division of the sexes on the culture: '. . . the shtetl sees itself through the eyes of men and talks about itself through the words of men. It is set up as a man's culture with women officially subordinate and officially inferior. The men greet each day by offering thanks to God "that Thou has not made me a woman".'[17]

Although the home was considered the respected domain of women and the observance of rigid religious practices was demanded of them, they were, after marriage, utterly consumed by childbearing, the preparation and serving of food and the intricate arrangements needed for the celebration of the festivals. As everything they did was considered a duty and a necessity they received little gratitude or thanks. Since their marriages were based on the need to maintain family life and not on any inter-personal relationship, they found little understanding or consideration from their husbands. They became wholly dependent emotionally on their children, relating especially to their sons who by comparison rated so much higher, that their need to drain love from them became an obsession. Diamond, who looked closely at these relationships, writes:

. . . the mother's relationship with her son, most strikingly in his early years, was direct and over-protective, with particular overattention to feeding. She did her best to smother him with love, as she conceived it, to cushion him against an alien and threatening environment. Undoubtedly, the mother's response to the son served as an outlet also for emotionally inhibited relationships with the symbol-saturated father. She strove to keep the son a child, her child, an object of affection, a release from maternal-female emotions that were too often abused in other spheres of activity. She cherished this boy and surrendered him reluctantly to the social process that would convert him into another male, another Jew, another husband who would take another wife bearing other sons. But until then he belonged briefly and exclusively to her as her husband never could. We can, I think, view this relationship of the Jewish mother to her son as a species of romance, cultivated, cherished and idealised by the mother. For her the contact with the son represented an oasis of spontaneous emotion in a desert of duties.[18]

Because women learned their ritualized duties by rote and through the oral tradition, they were offered no rational explanations for rites they performed. As a result, they were heavily steeped in mysticism, superstition and fear. 'There is a shtetl population of demons, spirits and witches,' Zborowski and Herzog observe.[19] They were constantly occupied with warding off the evil eye in whose grip they were powerfully held. While the men pursued their religious fanaticism through a rational approach based on an understanding of its philosophy and dynamics, the women were denied this. Their lives were narrow, circumscribed, undignified, bitter and hard. And there seemed to be no way in which they could be released from this oppression. They were allowed none of the tools of emancipation and knew of no other experiences or possibilities. They were constantly under threat in their homes from pogroms and other forms of carnage, yet they were given no means of defending themselves. The men's preoccupation with religious observance absolved them from their responsibilities towards the women and children but at the same time they did not recognize that the women were without tools and skills to protect themselves. This inconsistancy is illustrated by Zborowski and Herzog:

> As full participants in the burden of economic support the women escape the burden of a sheltered life. If anyone is sheltered it is the scholarly man. Women and girls move freely ... everyone assumes she can take care of herself and even though an extremely high stake is set on her womanly virtue there is no over-weening fear that she will not be able to preserve her own.[20]

The unreality of this expectation was born out by the disastrous treatment of the women during the pogroms. Describing events in Eastern Europe in 1881 and wishing to draw the attention of the British public to the behaviour of the Russians towards the Jews, *The Times* of Wednesday 11 January 1882, in a long article, reported:

> Next day, similar scenes of violence occurred at Bowary in the neighbourhood of Kieff in the province of Czenizow. On the same day, still more disgraceful deeds were expected at Beresowka in the province of Cherson. Here, lust seemed more a principal motive than plunder. While the Jews of the village were at synagogue a mob

attacked the Jewesses and violated many of them, causing the death of these, others who escaped the worse evil were driven into the river and nine ultimately died from the effects of the exposure.

During the first half of the nineteenth century the only release from this misery for a woman was to elope with a Gentile. This meant liberation from the shtetl but it also meant total rejection by parents and family, for a daughter who married a non-Jew was considered to have died. Her name was never again mentioned in the home or in the village. To accept this degree of disapproval was a searing experience. The price of emancipation was agonizing.[21]

But inevitably changes came. The events of the Crimean War (1854–6) and the death of Tsar Nicholas in 1855 brought Russia into closer touch with the rest of Europe which, in turn, began to undergo great economic and social changes. Although not as advanced as Britain and France, the lands of Eastern Europe were, with the ending of serfdom, undergoing an agrarian transformation. This, together with the extension of the railways and improvements in administration, brought about an easing in the lives of the Russian people. In 1861 the Government proclaimed a general emancipation of the peasants and created a climate which led to a degree of liberation for Jews. By the 1870s they moved about more freely and began to settle outside the Pale.

This relaxation of tension by the authorities caused the young men and women of the Pale to break away and settle in the surrounding towns of Kiev, Odessa, etc. By the end of the nineteenth century large communities of Jews looking for alternative lifestyles were living in towns away from home. Baron writes:

In 1884, there already were twelve cities of over 100,000 population in the Empire. Sixteen years later their number increased to sixteen. Next to the two capitals,[22] the largest of these were Warsaw, Odessa, Lodz, Riga, Kiev, Kharkov, Vilna, Ekaterinoslav and Kristiniev, each of which had a sizeable Jewish community. Odessa, Ekaterinoslav and Kiev where Jews started to settle – or resettle – under Russian domination showed the most substantial growth. The Odessa community embraced only 246 Jews in 1795, it grew to 17,000 in 1855, 138,915 in 1897 and 152,364 in 1904 ... Kiev ... had 207 Jews in 1797, 3,013 in 1863, 31,801 in 1897 and 50,792 in 1910.[23]

In this new environment they learned skills, developed political and social consciousness, changed their ways of life, dressed as town people and broadened their horizons. Shapiro writes: 'By ending the system whereby Jews in Russian schools had hitherto been subjected to official proselytizing pressure he (Alexander II) opened up the road from the ghettoes to the universities and hence to the professions.'[24]

They began to shed their strong religious ties and superstitions and started to integrate with the outside world. Throughout, small numbers of Jews had continuously left the shtetl, illegally, for America, France and England. As this trickle became a deluge towards the end of the nineteenth century, the cross-fertilization of ideas, drifting back and forth through letters and on the lips of travellers became international. 'The only hope of salvation lay in flight,'[25] wrote Golding, and Baron states:

'During the entire half century of 1820 to 1870 some 7,500 Russian and Polish Jews settled in the United States. During the decade 1871–80 the number rose to 40,000. In the following decade it increased to 135,000; from 1891–1900 it rose to 279,811 and between 1901–10 to 704,245.'[26]

As the new town-dwelling Jews found their independence and an independent voice, their excursions into political thought led them towards socialism, communism, anarchism and revolution. Greenberg writes:

In the early seventies, with the growth of a Jewish student body which came in closer contact with the Russian intelligensia, the number of Jewish revolutionaries increased considerably. But it was as Russians concerned with the plight of the Russian people, particularly the peasantry and not as Jews engaged in the battle for Jewish rights that these students joined the revolutionary movement.[27]

'Jewish revolutionaries participated in every phase of revolutionary activity. In the early seventies when the slogan of the revolution was "Go to the people", Jews also took part in this crusade to propagandize the peasantry.'[28] Even before this spread of liberalization in the country, Talmon tells us:

At that very time [1848–9][29] the problem of Jews and revolution began to assume truly vital significance in the Empire of the Czars.

All-comprehensive bondage on the one hand and the Messianic dis-position of the Russian people on the other, fed here a vision of total redemption through total revolution; that yearning could not but affect, most deeply, young Jewish men and women striving to enter the great stream of humanity but hemmed in on all sides by sustained and deliberately humiliating oppression.[30]

Only later did political consciousness of a particularly Jewish nature begin to express itself. This was manifested in the form-ation of the *Bund*, the General Jewish Workers Union of Lith-uania, Poland and Russia, founded in 1897. This Movement, 'came to serve as a decompression chamber, intermediate between social action within Jewry alone and the ampler stage of supra-national or "all-Russian" politics',[31] Vital writes and continues:

Overwhelmingly, even for revolutionaries, there was no question of dropping out of the Jewish community. It was rather that the forms in which Jewish particularism and national feelings had come increas-ingly to be conceived by virtually all adherents to the drive for the modernization of Jewish life in these closing years of the century was not religious and legal, as had been traditional in the past, but secular and literary. There was, thus, set a loose framework of loyalties and goals in which all radical movements evolved and of which all par-took.[32]

Thus it was that of the year 1903 Shapiro wrote: 'Jews formed seven million of a total population of 136 million ... about fifty per cent of the membership of the revolutionary parties were Jewish.'[33]

One of the radical movements into which some of these revo-lutionaries were seduced was one directed at creating a national home for the Jews in Palestine. Not yet called 'Zionism' it quickly came to be seen as a means of providing an answer to op-pression.[34] Some of those in this early movement had interpreted their miserable existence as being yet another manifestation of a long history of suppression, intolerance and hardship, that history culminating in the bad pogroms of 1881 and the May Laws. The events of 1881 had demonstrated the lack of solidarity between the peasants and the Jews and had disillusioned them. They began to feel that a national home would mean self-determinism, relief from oppression and a nationhood offering the possibilities for individual expression. For others, however, the behaviour of the shtetl was in itself an incitement to revolutionary thought. Spiro notes this.

It will be remembered that the vatikim when members of the Youth Movement[35] were in rebellion against the Jewish culture of the shtetl, as well as against the bourgeois culture of the European cities. And among the many aspects of these cultures that they wished to change were the 'false' sexual morality of the city, the 'partriarchal' authority of the male, the 'dependance' of the child on his father and the 'subjection of women'.[36]

At that stage the 'Zionist' movement offered nothing specific to women and the women were not yet ready to demand anything specific of it. It did offer them, however, the opportunity to leave the shtetl and to help mould a country which might serve them better.

The women who had broken out of the shtetl were different from their sisters who had remained behind. They had, somehow, found the strength and the motivation to uproot themselves and had been unable to suppress for ever their deep yearning for freedom, self-actualization and a greater degree of individuality. As they developed political consciousness alongside the men, they were soon as involved as their brothers. Isaac Bashevis Singer, in his novels,[37] alludes to their revolutionary zeal and Amos Elon tells us of Manya Shochat[38] who,

... had achieved some notoriety in Russian revolutionary circles by running arms for the anarchists and participating in clandestine plots and agitations. Once, as a twenty-year-old anarchist in Russia, she shot a Tsarist spy to death, dismembered his corpse, placed the pieces in a suitcase and sent it off by rail to a non-existent address in Siberia.[39]

And Greenberg writes: 'Another Russian Jewish political émigré, Anna Rosenstein, under the adopted name of Kuleshov, together with her husband Turati, organized the Italian Socialist Party. She also founded and edited for thirty-five years the central organ of the party, *Kritica Sociale*.'[40]

While for some, leaving the shtetl meant a fresh, if hard, start in the New World and an opportunity to seek a fortune (or, at

least, a rich husband of their own choice), for others it opened up
possibilities for understanding what had been happening to them
for so many decades, and for looking at the wider implications
involved. Greenberg writes: 'In the eighties, there existed a
number of socialist circles scattered throughout the Pale. In these
secret circles, which were really study groups, the workers taught
reading, writing, arithmetic, the natural sciences and the elementary principles of socialism.'[41] Those who had joined the left-wing
political groups saw international working-class solidarity as
offering ways of eliminating anti-semitism. For others, complete
assimilation and denial of their Jewishness was the answer, but for
others again, Zionistic concepts seemed to hold out the most hope
for the future. With such concepts they could remain Jews, socialists, and have a land of their own and return to a form of life
denied them by the existence of the Pale of Settlement which
offered artificial solutions and attempted to dehumanize them.
Rolbant says: 'The sons and daughters of the second Aliyah who
left behind them memories of the Czarist Régime were determined
that capitalism with its attendant evils of degration, poverty and
war should not provide a framework for the new society which
they sought to found in the Holy Land.'[42]

Gradually, as ideas about a national home grew, small groups of
radical Jews left for the physical privations of life in Palestine. Of
those early days in Palestine Laqueur writes:

> Everything was strange and unfamiliar – the people, the landscape,
> the whole atmosphere ... Living conditions were incredibly primitive
> even by eastern European standards. The newcomers lived in tents or
> miserable huts. They had to put up with malaria, snakes, scorpions,
> various bugs, overseers who made work hell, and a cultural environ-
> ment which was either Levantine or reminded them of the shtetl
> which they had left behind.[43]

It would be wrong, therefore, to give the impression that for
women ideas of emancipation and liberation were well thought
out or close to the surface or that they went with a definite philosophy of female equality and a revolutionary fervour for a
change of sex roles. Laqueur notes, 'The second immigration
wave[44] consisted mainly of individuals rather than groups. Not a
few had come to the country by mere accident, having joined

friends or relations without exactly knowing where they were going or why.'[45] Of Manya Shochat we read again: 'Her conversion to Zionism was almost an accident. Her worried family invented a sick brother in Palestine and in 1914 induced the twenty-five-year-old firebrand[46] to pay him a short visit. Dismayed at discovering the ruse upon her arrival she was nevertheless induced to remain in Palestine. She played a prominent role in the early pioneer society.'[47] Of her feminist sympathies we have no knowledge from this source. Amos Elon chronicles one, though, who was sure of her commitment. This was Rachel Ben Zvi, the wife of Israel's first President:

Rachel Ben Zvi was a pioneer and a political figure in her own right. She played a prominent role in Zionist affairs from the time she first arrived in the country in 1908. Even before that, despite her relative youth she had been a veteran of underground socialist and Zionist work in Czarist Russia. At the age of seventeen she had been arrested by the Russian police for participating in a clandestine socialist meeting. At her release from prison more than a year later, her apprehensive father had assured the director of the prison, 'I promise you, sir, that she will stay out of trouble from now on. We will keep her home.' But the young girl had broken in, 'No, I will not' ... in 1908, she later recalled she was sitting with her books in the Hermitage library,[48] when she was suddenly seized by so strong a desire to become a pioneer girl in Palestine that she left her books on the table and ran home, packed her things and took the first train south. At the Black Sea port of Odessa, while waiting for a boat, she encountered Chaim Nachman Bialik, the leading Hebrew poet of the time and a resident of Odessa. Bialik asked her, 'But what will you do in Palestine?' She answered him, 'I will live.'[49]

Amos Elon does not record her feminist leanings but Rachel Yanait Ben Zvi later became a founder of the Pioneer Women's Movement and devoted much of her time to developing vocational training for women.

This then was the background from which they came, these women who later became the pioneers of Israel. This environment had moulded them for generations and it was this environment which they had to fight before they could find liberty.

2. First, Second and Third *Aliyah*

'Excuse me, Gottlieb, aren't you a member of the Workers' Council, I was told to apply to you for work. I want to start tomorrow morning.' 'There's no ladies' work.' 'I don't want "ladies' work". I'll do any kind. They told me workers are needed here; that's why I came.' 'I don't know. The colonists don't want girls.' 'But you're making a mistake. I'm not looking for girls' work. Are you afraid I won't make good? Give me a chance. If I don't get through the regulation amount, take it off my pay.' 'I'll see. Come in tomorrow.'[1]

Equality of opportunity and liberation for those Eastern European Jewesses were not won in their lifetime. The small group of men and women who went to Palestine in the first wave of immigration (1880–95) and their compatriots who arrived in the Second (1905–14) and the Third (1919–25) *Aliyah*, embued as they might have been with thoughts of egalitarianism and humanism, had little opportunity of fulfilling their ambitions. For the first and second wave, arrival and establishment in the Land of Israel meant gruelling hard work and severe deprivation. They had to return to the first principles of survival in a physically difficult and alien country. 'Problems such as the state of women workers; the joint bringing up of children ... have not been resolved,'[2] wrote Viteles of those early pioneers. And of the hardship Ben Gurion writes:

Bitter and frequent were the birth pangs of farm settlement in Israel. Plagues of nature, the desolation of the terrain, Arab enmity, corrupt Turkish administration, antagonism from the zealots of the 'old Yishuv' in Jerusalem, the agricultural ignorance of all but a few settlers ... No one today can even begin to comprehend the grand sweep of purpose, the vision, the dedication, demanded of those pathfinders.'[3]

While they were struggling for life, two thousand miles away in Europe the newly forming Zionist movement was developing along different lines from those self-sacrificing pioneers. In Switzerland, France and Germany, members of the Jewish intelligensia were organizing themselves to take control of the power base of these dedicated, ideological *chalutzim*. The self-proclaimed leader of this movement, Theodore Herzl, was creating strategies and policies unrelated to the wishes and needs of the pioneers but based on his own private needs and motivation. Amos Elon writes: 'Herzl, somewhat naïvely, hoped to transplant into the proposed Jewish homeland, his own sophisticated milieu of witty intellectuals, bohemians and philosopher-businessmen; he did not envisage the structural changes, the social and cultural revolution postulated by the leftish Zionists of Russia.'[4] Whether Herzl's hopes were naïve is open to conjecture for he was, nevertheless, able to carry with him large numbers of armchair Zionists who supported him and built him up as a leader. His brain child, the first World Zionist Congress held in Basel, Switzerland, in 1897, laid the foundations for the Zionist movement as it has developed until today. That Congress, which was attended by men and women from all over the world, although those in Palestine were not present, became the mouthpiece for world Zionism, yet women were denied the right to vote.[5]

In spite of the importance of the Congress and its significance for the future of Zionism, its ambience and content bore little relation to the immediacy of the lives of the settlers in Palestine with their high ideals and revolutionary fervour. Writing of Herzl's efforts to assemble the Congress Vital writes:

> The deepest reservations in the East concerned Herzl's methods ... the 'noise' he made, the opportunities he gave the anti-Semitic press to publish canards, the neglect of what was modest and practical as opposed to an evident tendency to the grand and the ambitious: and underlying them were old, mostly unspoken fears, of the dangerous man, the false prophet, the new Shabbetai Zevi[6] who would stimulate unsatisfiable wants, loose the bonds of the Law and of authority, and end by leading the innocents to catastrophe.[7]

An exponent of the earlier 'Lovers of Zion' movement which had inspired the first wave of settlers, Ahad Ha'am,[8] attended that first Congress and wrote in 1897:

There has been a revolution in their world. It is no longer 'Love of Zion (*Hibbat Zion*)' but 'Zionism (*Zioniyuth*)'. Indeed there are even 'precisionists' who use only the European form of the name (*Zionismus*) – thus announcing to all and sundry that they are not talking about anything so antiquated as Hibbat Zion, but about a new, up-to-date movement which comes, like its name, from the West, where people are innocent of the Hebrew language.[9]

That battle, over the re-interpretation of the same ideology, was the first of many which occurred during the First and Second *Aliyah* and which served to dominate the lives of the settlers.

The movement which developed in Palestine grew out of the spontaneous wishes and desires of the settlers and was, in fact, in opposition to the wishes of the Zionists in Europe. 'When the Palestinians[10] began to found co-operative agricultural settlements, they had to face bitter resistance,'[11] Laqueur writes. This 'bitter resistance' came mainly from the newly forming left-wing political parties but also from the Zionist Movement itself which did not understand the concept.

... the idea of permanent settlements on the Communist pattern, dispensing with private property, was thought to be fantastic. When Manya Wilbushewitch, one of the early pioneers, talked about it to Max Nordau[12] in Paris, she was told that she was suffering from feverish delusions and was advised to consult a psychiatrist colleague.[13]

The concept of working the land collectively came directly from the imagination and initiative of Manya Wilbushewitch and her comrades, encouraged and influenced by cooperative theories of Professor Franz Oppenheimer[14] and others. These concepts, which aimed at producing progressive life styles for these revolutionary pioneers and which brought about the founding of the first kibbutzim, were based on equality and were committed to female emancipation. 'Even at that time, in the early years of the twentieth century, the young women understood that, in order to build in the land a new, revolutionary and egalitarian society, special attention would have to be given to the status of the women in society and at work.'[15]

Throughout the period the women pioneers organized and reorganized themselves into working groups fighting constantly to be accepted as equal. Rebecca Danith described her experiences at the beginning of the First World War.

Three months later the Federation of Labour undertook the work on the Tiberias road. The Government had ordered the colonists of Galilee to prepare gravel, and the colonists turned over the work to the Federation. It was a contract job and so the first group went out for a week to break stones and to determine at the same time what the price should be. It was with the utmost difficulty that I, a woman, could persuade the comrades to take me along. There were all sorts of objections. The work was too much for a girl; it wasn't nice for a Jewish girl to be working on the open road. There was even one comrade who believed that it would be a national crime! But I and another girl stuck it out for the first week and, in spite of renewed objections stayed on. At the end of the first month there was a whole group of women at work on the road.[16]

And Spiro writes: '... the Youth Movement, from which many kibbutz values are derived, were strongly feminist in orientation.'[17] Also, they were seen as providing a basis for a society based on socialist principles. 'The spiritual renaissance of the woman in Palestine is part of the spring movement of the entire people, it has to do with Zionism, with pioneering, with work on the earth, with the rediscovery of the old–new land and the old–new language, with socialist ideals,' wrote Rachel Kateznelson-Rubashow in the book *The Plough Woman*, published in 1932.[18] Yet such ideas began to founder from the beginning. Elon writes:

There were other differences between the more unworldly Second Aliyah Colonists[19] and those who were emerging as their leaders. An important contrast was the growing sense of pragmatism on the part of Ben Zvi[20] and Ben Gurion.[21] As early as 1909, while others were practising the 'religion of labour',[22] Ben Zvi and Ben Gurion helped to organize a secret defense organisation.[23]

He writes also, 'Looking back in later years he (Ben Gurion) claimed that within a few hours of his first arrival in the country he had already lost patience with "meaningless abstract talk".'[24]

Thus the fact that feminist objectives were beginning to be lost sight of was not entirely the fault of the pioneers, for it must be recognized that they were only part of the wider Zionist movement and that they were caught up in the ideology of Western Zionism.

The Jews of Palestine, at that time, became engulfed in two other matters which were allowed to take precedence over the personal and spiritual needs of the settlers. One was self-defence, and particularly defence of the *kibbutzim*, many of which were in out-lying areas and were therefore thought to be exceedingly vulnerable to attack. The other was the complicated political games being played by the male leaders of the Zionist movement in the Diaspora. At first there was the need to be defended against threats, real or imagined, from their neighbours and then, after 1914, from both the British and the Arabs in a more organized way. In 1909 a self-styled defence organization calling itself *Hashomer* emerged. This group soon established itself as an authoritarian organization with strong para-military connotations. The climate for such activities grew out of the general lawlessness of the country and the 'corrupt and effete Turkish administration'.[25] As a result they were able to take over and control the defence of the Jewish settlements. Working as a 'semi-conspiratorial nucleus'[26] they were not always admired by the settlers who wanted to find peaceful answers to their problems and who were not convinced of the hostility of their Arab neighbours. Fundamentally pacifist they, nevertheless, came to rely on these uncontrolled groups who roamed the countryside on their behalf.

The 'success' of the watchmen proved the start of a downhill slide into violence against the wishes of many settlers. These guarding groups earned a reputation for bravery and heroism and built up a romantic legend about themselves, one which was easily maintained given the adulatory attitudes to young men, traditional in Jewish life. But as Perlmutter points out,

> The revolutionaries of Hashomer were not content to maintain this 'heroic' organization simply as a union of valorous watchmen, as they were fully aware of the opportunities open to them for infiltrating 'defenceless' social-democratic groups. What they needed to accomplish this objective was a military élite and a socio-economic base to support it.[27]

Because of its conspiratorial nature the chalutzim had little opportunity to oppose them or to keep track of all the decisions which Hashomer was making. It had set itself up to 'establish the dictatorship of an agrarian proletariat based in fortified collectives and was to serve as a vanguard of the Socialist–Zionist movement'.[28]

By 1912 Hashomer had drawn up

Proposals for the protection of the Yishuv which set out four aims:
1. Hashomer will not limit its role to physical protection of the Jewish settlements; it must inculcate into these people the consciousness that they must defend themselves.
2. Hashomer must provide the nucleus for the widening of the defensive functions of the Jewish community.
3. Hashomer has to have a monopoly over the defence of the Jewish community of Palestine.
4. Therefore, Hashomer must serve as the professional-conspiratorial armed force of the Yishuv.
    'To accomplish these objectives,' Perlmutter writes, 'Hashomer, acting as a secret society also established the organisational and procedural paraphernalia for such activity.'[29]

In charting the development of the new community it is vital to record that Hashomer was an unrestrained anarchic, violent gang which set the pattern for future Israeli defence behaviour. Koestler writes, 'These "Watchmen", . . . were a kind of Hebrew cowboy or Wild West ranger . . . These Jewish Buffalo Bills were the forerunners of Haganah.'[30] They also, slowly, laid the seeds which shifted the ideology from one of deep commitment to the land, peaceful settlement and a radical change of lifestyle for all, to one of violence, defence and male superiority.

On the other hand, in the developed Western world the Zionist moguls pursued their own political ends, gaining status and influence as Zionists where they might otherwise have remained nonentities. Even David Ben Gurion, Israel's first Prime Minister, had little experience of working life in Palestine when he started to pursue the leadership. Laqueur writes,

Aware that their education had been incomplete, Ben Gurion and Ben Zvi decided to study at the University of Constantinople, where they met David Remes.[31] Later on, Sharett[32] and Dov Hos[33] also went to the Turkish capital. Shlomo Zemach[34] went to Paris and

Salman Shazar[35] to Germany to study philosophy and history; both returned only after the end of the First World War. By the early 1920s, ten years after they had arrived in Palestine, almost all of them had become party or trade union officials. The iron law of élitism and bureaucratization in political movements had again prevailed.[36]

The women of the First and Second Aliyah were soon to discover that they were not engaged in a struggle of their own choice. Even the climate of Zionist pioneering did not favour them. The settlers were mostly young people and the Zionist groups which sponsored them did not encourage women to join the shipments. Tiger and Shepher write: 'the proportion of men over women among the founders of the first kibbutzim was very high, as it was in the rest of Palestine's Jewish population. Some of the early settlements consisted of a dozen young men and one or two women. Later more women arrived, but a disproportionate ratio persisted almost until the establishment of the state.'[37] The leaders in Europe who bought and owned the land were without understanding of practical requirements, unrealistic and devoid of concern for individuals. The pioneers were perceived as being without sexual needs and beyond the boundaries of human necessities. Spiro writes:

When these people in their late teens and early twenties arrived in Palestine, they were confronted with the problem of establishing their own sexual morality and this task was not easy. 'It was difficult,' commented a vattika, 'from an erotic point of view.' The sex ratio was 2:1 – sixty males and thirty females – which was difficult enough. In addition, they were supposed to live together as one community but not as couples. 'It is little wonder that we were all,' as she put it, 'concerned with sex.'[38]

Yet, the early settlers were expected to be puritanical, abstemious and self-controlled.

For those settlers who were able to survive the early hardships there was little opportunity for developing ideas of emancipation. Writing of Degania, the first collective settlement in Palestine, Joseph Baratz, one of its founders, states:

All of us, men and women alike, had come to Palestine with the same aim of changing our lives through and through. Here, we thought, the woman would find freedom and equality in tilling the soil beside her brothers. But the group that had gone up ... numbering twelve souls, included only two women – just the number needed for the domestic work ... it must be confessed that the men were still psychologically unprepared for the radical step of allowing the women to work in the fields ... This attitude on the part of the men made it difficult for the women to secure their rights.[39]

Although there had clearly been talk of equality of the sexes from the very beginning of the new movement, both in Eastern Europe and in Palestine itself, it appeared rarely to have become more than that.

This attitude did not go unnoticed by the women who were quick to describe it themselves. Zipporah Bar-Droma writes,

In Palestine there came a parting of the ways. Over there, in the Russian exile, men and women had been equal comrades in the movement. We worked together, suffered together in the prisons and in the remote countries to which we were expelled; the moment the first pioneer certificates reached us, admitting us into Palestine, we were divided into the two classes: men comrades and women comrades.

The very first instructions we got from Palestine hinted at this inequality, and when we landed we were actually separated into two groups. In the one group were those who were 'building the country'; in the other were those who would take care, in every-day matters, of 'the builders of the country'. And always we hear the same formula: 'This piece of work will need so many men, and the men will employ so many women...'[40]

· The beginnings of family life in the kibbutzim added to the problem. Because these young people from the shtetl were anxious not to repeat earlier behavioural patterns, children were born outside marriage and they became, at everyone's request, the responsibility of the whole community. Bettelheim writes:

To the founding woman, her mother's life seemed so overwhelming an example of giving to children, so much all of one piece, that she could not imagine herself identifying with parts of it and not others. These mothers of theirs, in their singleminded devotion to family and children, seemed most powerful figures to their daughters. To be free of such an image, one had to be free of it *in toto*. The daughter could not conceive in her unconscious of being able to take care of husband

and children and still be an equal companion to men. She felt she could not do that much better than her mother. But she felt she could do things entirely differently. If her mother's life had been all of a piece, all wifely and motherly, so would her life be all of a piece. She would be solely man's equal companion at work and in her whole daily life.[41]

Throughout the whole period of the growth of the Yishuv, the immigrants who had come to settle the land had little say or control over their lives. The Turkish administration cared little for what went on within the country itself and the immigrants' only reference group was the Zionist Movement, still situated in Western Europe and dominated by Theodore Herzl and his followers. This movement, entirely male-controlled and devoted to the establishment of its own version of a Jewish State, was not concerned with, nor sensitive to, the needs and aspirations of the people of Palestine. Later of the relationship between the Jews and Arabs[42] (a not unimportant area of consideration) Laqueur writes:

The few Jews who devoted so much thought and effort to relations with their Arab neighbours were a source of bewilderment and irritation to their less self-conscious brethren. Berl Katznelson,[43] who was both the conscience and *éminence gris* of the Zionist Labour movement, relates how shocked he was to discover that the question which pre-occupied German chalutzim was not the plight of their brothers left behind, not the Jews facing extinction in Hitler's expanding Reich, but the problem of the Arab workers.[44]

The Zionist Movement itself was concerned mainly with influencing Western power centres and fulfilling personal ambitions. Few of Israel's political leaders before the First World War and until the signing of the Balfour Declaration in 1917, when ideas for the State were being formed, had lived long in Palestine and even fewer had been involved in developing the land and the country. 'Looking back, fifty years after the publication of the Balfour Declaration,' writes Ben Gurion, 'I must say regretfully that the Zionist leadership of that period, which was undoubtedly a great period in the history of the Jewish people, did not pay proper attention to the main internal task.'[45] He goes on, 'Dr Weizmann (Israel's first President) had not yet assumed a central role in the Zionist Movement. He was constantly aware of the need for labour and settlement . . . and was one of the few Zionist leaders who saw the necessity, during the Turkish régime of 1907–8, of visiting Israel.'[46]

The arrival of Ben Zvi, Ben Gurion and others created new pressures as they began to form the Palestinian Poale Zion Party[47] and single-mindedly and ruthlessly began their domination of the society. This, in rivalry with the established Hapoel Hatzair[48] group, which was growing at the same time, caused continuing political battles. It is not the place here to discuss these battles or to comment on the two parties, except in so far as they hindered the struggles of the women to achieve status and recognition. Laqueur writes:

> By 1914, the number of Jewish workers had risen to about sixteen hundred; by that time yet a third party had come into existence, the 'non-partisans' who preferred not to join any of the existing groups. There were also several hundred workers of Yemenite[49] origin who stayed out of the violent and to them incomprehensible quarrels of their European brothers.[50]

As for the women, they had little hope of fulfilling their dreams. The daily life of everyone in Palestine was hard and there was little time or energy for the full discussion and consolidation of new ideas. Malaria and typhus were endemic, much of the country was either swamp or desert and they had come without agricultural or horticultural skills. Gradually, the women found themselves losing ground. Though they had arrived filled with a new sense of purpose they were gradually and systematically relegated to women's work and service jobs. Talmon writes: 'Frequent pregnancies and confinements removed women from regular work. An increase in the number of children entailed the transfer of a growing number of workers to services and child care and significantly lowered the number of workers in productive labour.'[51] This even though children's houses were set up in the kibbutzim from the earliest days to free the women from constantly caring for their children. This was essential if women looking after the children were to spend some time with their own children. Laqueur writes: 'Most male members of the kibbutzim were engaged in agricultural work. It was far more difficult to provide "productive" employment for the women, who were heavily concentrated on work in the kitchen and laundry, and, of course, the children's houses.'[52]

But the awareness of the women and their committed feminism did not influence the founders of Degania[53] and the other early kibbutzim, and they were not offered any kind of liberation. Although they helped to build Degania A in a real and positive way, it soon became clear that within this new social framework, the women's role remained largely the traditional one. Naava Eisin writes,

> Most women were assigned to work in the kitchen, the laundry or in the children's rooms. The principle difference on this plane between the women in the collective and the farmers wives in the old-style villages was that, under the new regime, instead of cooking and cleaning for one family – their own – the women in the kibbutz were obliged to feed and provide services to tens (later hundreds) of other families.[54]

Yet some were determined to have a say in the building of the country and to exercise their right to full participation in all manner of work – in the fields, in construction and in self-defence. The women of the Third Aliyah, anxious about what was happening to their dream, started to found women's farm settlements. These are described by Rachel Janaith,

> The *meshek ha-poaloth*, or women's farm settlement, has a distinct purpose; to prepare the women worker for the general *meshek* or farm settlement. But at first it had an additional purpose; it was a larger school life. There was an education value in the dividing up of the work, the sharing of responsibility and the adaptation of the individual to the group life. The meshek had to be self-supporting; and therefore the comrades in it had to take up all its economic problems. In such surroundings the character of the woman comrade set firm; she developed the necessary independence and initiative.[55]

The women trained on this farm and others like them became an important part of the labour force. However, their role was soon undermined. In the years 1926 to 1927 severe unemployment brought hunger and suffering. The women of the newly formed women's settlements managed to work and to eat, but the women outside, who had no training and no status, were jobless. As a result of the growth of factories and workshops these unskilled women workers poured into the towns to find work at the sewing machine, the loom and in domestic service – traditional female jobs – where they worked in pitiable conditions for wretched pay. Deeply resentful, they kept up their battle for equality, as Tiger and Shepher note, but the pressures were too strong.

'But whatever the argument, women succumbed to the same course of events. Under the demand for expanded services for a growing population they gradually left the agricultural branches; they fought hard, but succeeded only in delaying the change for a while.'[56] As a result of not being able to keep up with changing skills, e.g. the developments in machinery and equipment in agriculture and industry, their value and worth in these areas diminished. To illustrate their position the story is told that, when on a newly formed settlement, the first cow was acquired the women begged to be allowed to milk her. In order to have this privilege, they offered to take on many other menial tasks, but were told that the cow would not provide as much milk if milked by a woman!

The women of the Third Aliyah, fresher and stronger in their commitment to equality – not yet ground down by the impossible system which had defeated their forerunners – joined the 'labour battalions'[57] and formed cooperatives to undertake the hard public works which were essential to develop the country. Nevertheless, they had to fight for the right to crush rocks and make gravel, to climb high scaffolds and to work at any and every task necessary. And, as previously, when work became more scarce they soon found themselves elbowed out as priority for existing jobs went to the men. Nationally, their contribution went unnoticed, for Elon notes:

In later years, even brief membership in the select fraternity of men who had paved, say, the Haifa–Jedda or the Afula–Nazareth roads, became a note of aristocratic distinction and frequently a key to political advancement. In 1954, thirty years after the event and six after the attainment of independence, almost half the leading politicians in the ruling labour party and a third of all senior officials in government, in the trade unions, in the nationalized or union-owned industries, had been, in the twenties, construction workers, labourers in road gangs, or members of bizarre communes, near mystic brother-hoods of men in rags deliriously serving an idea. Few would have suspected in them the budding cells of a future power elite.'[58]

During the twenties and thirties the women's discontent and frustration grew. Little of this has been published in English and diaries of women of that time are not available to every re-searcher. However, they are hinted at in various publications, in-cluding Golda Meir's autobiography which reveals the lack of understanding and sympathy given to these women fighting for their freedom. In the book *My Life*, she writes, of her experiences shortly after her arrival in Merhavia, the kibbutz on which she lived:

Let me explain that, in those days, kibbutz women hated kitchen duty, not because it was hard (compared with other work on the settlements it was rather easy) but because they felt it to be de-meaning. Their struggle wasn't for equal 'civic' rights, which they had in abundance, but for equal burdens. They wanted to be given whatever work their male comrades were given – paving roads, hoeing fields, building houses, or standing guard duty – not to be treated as though they were different and automatically relegated to the kitchen ... I couldn't for the life of me understand what all the fuss was about and said so ... I remained more concerned with the quality of our diet than with 'feminine emancipation'.[59]

And she continues:

When my turn came to work on Saturday morning, I figured as follows: we have no oil, sugar or eggs so let's add more water and a little flour and make a lot of cookies, enough for Friday night and Saturday breakfast, too. At first, this was regarded as being 'counter-revolutionary' but after a while everyone quite liked the idea of cookies twice a week – for the same money. My most celebrated 'bour-geois' contribution, however, – about which settlers all over the Emek talked disparagingly for months – was the 'tablecloth' (made from a sheet) that I spread on the table for Friday night suppers – with a centrepiece of wild flowers, yet! The members of Merhavia sighed, grumbled and warned me that I was giving the kibbutz a bad name, but they let me have my way.[60]

By the end of the 1920s the women's frustrations were clearly identifiable, yet ignored. In 1929 and 1930 Ada Maimon published two books recording these frustrations and the inability of the kibbutz women to fulfil their expectations. Women were becoming invisible.

3. The Birth of Chauvinism

As the settlers and the settlements became more established the towns began to expand. Between 1923 and 1926, for example, the population of Tel Aviv rose from sixteen to forty thousand. It was a time of great political and social activity and the Balfour Declaration, signed by the British Government in 1917, virtually guaranteed those in control of Palestine a national home for the Jewish people.

Before the advent of the Third Aliyah the country, which was largely agrarian, had been mainly concerned with immediate domestic problems but 'by 1920', Laqueur writes, 'labour gradually became a major social and political factor and its representatives entered the executive of bodies of Palestinian Jewry'.[1] And from this labour force women were beginning to be excluded. By 1926 the distribution of working women was as follows: 1,500 women working in farming, 800 in the colonies, 400 in the workers' and general kitchens, 200 in sundry occupations, 800 in factories, 800 in offices, sewing rooms, hospitals and printshops, 150 in public works, and 400 as helpers in private homes. More than 1,500 young women were unemployed. The small proportion of women in direct labour ensured their lack of representation in the areas of power which were forming.[2]

In spite of the arrival of a new wave of settlers, the leadership of the country remained in the hands of Zionist pioneers like Ben Gurion, Ben Zvi, David Remes, Berl Katznelson, Sprinzak[3] – Zionists who had devoted their lives mainly to travel and study but had done little to help build the country on the ground. Although there was much talk of democracy, David Ben Gurion and Berl Katznelson 'frequently imposed their views upon the rest' (Laqueur) as political parties grew and the country formed the Histadrut[4] and the defence organizations of *Haganah* and *Irgun*

Zvai Leumi (the breakaway militia of the newly forming Revisi-
onist[5] party).

The Histadrut, formed in 1920, was the first official indication
that all was not well for women. Although it was agreed from the
beginning that women would have equal membership with men it
was seen at the first conference that women, who made up 50 per
cent of the membership, were seriously under-represented on the
various committees which were formed.

Gradually, growing unemployment and the drift to the towns
caused the women pioneers who had formed women's farm settlements to form groups in the towns to improve the working conditions of those women. In 1921 forty-three women delegates
representing 485 women attended a conference of working women
which laid the foundation for and later formed the Working
Women's Movement (*Moetzet Hapaelot*). The Movement was,
from its inception, committed to providing work for women and
undertook the task of broadening the range of occupational
branches which would accept women workers and that of giving
training for productive work. As a result the 'Women's Farms'
which were established gained status and recognition and the first
of a series of technical courses for women in the construction field
opened in Tel Aviv – a school for floor-tile layers. From here a
number of women were eventually accepted for employment in
the men's building-work gangs. Naava Eisin tells us:

> From the first Convention (and in practice until today) the
> members of the Working Women's Council continued in their efforts
> to strengthen the position of the working woman. In times of work
> shortage and unemployment they opposed the prevailing tendencies
> in favour of giving whatever opportunities there were to men, in
> preference to women workers. They defended the principle that a
> married woman is entitled to maintain herself and to contribute by
> her work to the welfare of the family, and not to be considered merely
> as a 'dependant' of the 'head of the family – the principal provider' –
> the familiar designation of the male.[6]

Clearly, this movement created whatever benefits women gained in
later years, but their concentration on such fundamental and life-
saving needs left them without time or energy to influence the
national scene politically, as the Histadrut was doing, at a time

when the country was moving in a direction which was to prove disastrous to women.

As fascism in Germany grew and the need for a safe refuge for Jews became urgent the conflict with the British Mandate grew more violent. Power centres and nation building moved away from the pioneers and their problems and focused on the para-military groups and the political leadership. Slowly the political arena switched from Western Europe to Palestine where the World Zionist Organisation, under the auspices of the British, set up the Jewish Agency[7] in 1929. At the same time the military wings of the various political parties, the Haganah on the left and the Irgun Zvai Leumi[8] on the right, were growing. Perlmutter writes:

Recognising the reluctance of the British to defend their settlements against Arab attack, the Jews used the situation as an excuse for buttressing their own defence forces. Working closely with the British, Zionist moderates were able to develop a clandestine Jewish army protected by the Mandatory but not responsible to it.[9]

The military achievements of the Haganah went hand-in-hand with the political achievement and leadership ambitions of Ben Gurion. So important did this seem that, in 1936, 'Funds from the World Zionist Organisation were allocated for the increased purchase of arms and weapons and for an elaborate, large-scale programme to train Palestinian youth as the core of a future army.'[10] Elsewhere Perlmutter writes that:

The 1930s were years of growing power for Socialist–Zionism ... Concurrently, the organisational growth of Histadrut was greatly enhanced by the rise of Haganah, the defence establishment it sustained and sheltered. Despite the fact that it was a clandestine and limited operation Haganah became a major institution in the entire Yishuv social system. It is not surprising that Histadrut's political critics called Haganah a 'state within a state'; it was (in fact) a political institution with institutional leaders and a professional staff, as were all Socialist–Zionist vehicles for advancing the development of a Jewish socialist commonwealth.[11]

While women had taken an important part in the various military groups of the Yishuv during the troubles of the 1930s they were given little credit for their efforts and were not honoured with positions of importance. Gradually they dropped away as an important factor in the war-machine. In the days of the Yishuv the Palmach,[12] the élite corps, consisted of both men and women, but women consistently took no share in the praise and applause. A clue to this discrepancy is supplied by Yigal Allon:

From the start girls were taken into the Palmach for active duty. In the beginning, they were given the same command training as their male counterparts and did the same course. But both the Palmach and the Haganah High Command worried about the possible aftermath of intensive combat training for women. The girls, for their part, stormed at any proposed discrimination, arguing that it ran counter to the spirit of the new society being built in Palestine to restrict women to domestic chores, particularly since they had proven their competence as marksmen and sappers. In the end the wider counsel prevailed; the girls were trained for combat, but placed in units of their own so that they would not compete physically with the men. Whenever possible, they were trained for defensive warfare only; Palmach women soldiers were used extensively as wireless operators, front line nurses, scouts and quartermasters though many also fought and died in battle.[13]

At this critical time for the Jews of Palestine the establishment of a viable fighting force created a basis for the nation-state. While the British Mandate ruled politically, and political decisions were being taken elsewhere, the growth of a serious fighting force became a symbol of potency for the aspiring nation. At last Jews were showing their strength and power. The men who had come from generations of emasculated manhood were at last fulfilling their deepest needs to assert themselves and gain recognition. Any success achieved by women in this field would have threatened this image. The men were fighting a private fight from which women were excluded.

The War of Liberation, when it came in 1948, estabished the Israel Defence Forces as leaders of the nation; it 'thrust the army into prominence and from that time on army leaders have been influential in the governmental and economic élites committed to rapid modernization'.[14] It is not the place here to discuss the details of that War or to take part in the debate surrounding it. But it is important to the women's cause in that it made specific the tone of the country and allowed the élitism of the fighting male Jew to take hold of the culture and mould the lives of the people. The country at that time was poor and undeveloped; there was little time for vaingloriousness and boasting. But those who had led the fighting were beginning to see themselves as the cream and to want positions of power and influence. As the war myths grew and stories of bravery were absorbed into the folk-lore little was heard of women. There are few recorded acts of bravery of women in that war; no memorials to women, no women generals, no record of women in the frontline. In their book *The Israeli Army*, Luttwak and Horowitz make slight mention of women's involvement in the early years. Yet, speaking to Israeli women of those times it is clear that their role was a real and important one for which they received and continue to receive no recognition.[15]

A major speech by Ben Gurion in the first Knesset[16] gave public confirmation of the inferior status of women which was to become institutionalized from this point on. The oft repeated duties of motherhood were given as the reason why women should be excluded from combat.

Now, for the question of women in the Army. When one discusses the position of women, two factors must be taken into consideration. First, women have a special mission as mothers. There is no greater mission in life, and nature has decreed that only a woman can give birth to a child. This is a woman's task and her blessing. However, a second factor must be remembered; the woman is not only a woman, but a personality in her own right in the same way as a man. As such, she should enjoy the same rights and responsibilities as the man, except where motherhood is concerned. There are members of this House who feel differently. That is their privilege, but the majority of the community accepts the basic principle that women cannot be allowed to occupy a lower position in society than men. The arguments heard here against taking women into the Army were heard thirty years ago from the Representatives of Mizrahi[17] when they opposed the participation of women in elections to the National Assembly.[18] They too appealed to tradition. Now the members of Mizrahi and of Agudat Israel[19] sit together with women in the Knesset and in the Government ... We have no intention of putting women into combat units, though no one can be sure that, should we be attacked and have to fight for our lives, we should not call on the service of every man and woman. But the law in question deals with a peacetime situation and we want to give women only the most basic military training.[20]

This decision, taken without serious consultation with women, had the effect of playing down their significance in the Armed Forces and disestablishing them from the centres of power and influence. It also seriously negated their role in the society and made it possible for Tom Bowden to write, disrespectfully, nearly thirty years later in 1976:

The girls – having been checked, surveyed by X-rays, vaccinated, graded, advised and finally wrapped in *chic* but practical new uniforms – are despatched to begin their twenty months of military service. The fundamental aim of basic training is to acclimatize the young recruits to the rigors and mores of army life ... especially for the girls, long hard days devoid of make-up and fine clothes ... Women's service quite simply increases the IDF's fighting manpower. Thus most girl soldiers can be found working happily as typists, secretaries and clerks in army bases throughout Israel – with prettier Chen[21] girls working for General Staff officers or in public relations work.[22]

As the Army replaced the synagogues and the yeshivot as the field of privilege, respect, honour, worship, it became sacred as the synagogue had once been and substituted its own form of strength, power and mysticism. Their lowly role in the armed forces ensured that women would not be included in this aura.

4. Independence for Whom?

After 1948 few of the early values remained. The male leaders of Israel had little vision. They were narrowly committed to a policy of immigration and defence as the only natural means of development and they pursued that policy with vigour. Immigration came not entirely from Europe and the United States, where feminist views were beginning to sprout, but from North Africa, Kurdistan, Turkey, Syria and Lebanon where Jews had remained backward, traditional and highly ritualistic. Lissak writes:

> The immigrants leaving for Palestine were small selective groups intent on creating a new type of Jewish society in their historical homeland, whereas the waves of immigration after 1948, particularly those from Muslim countries, encompassed whole Jewish populations whose social, economic and political basis for existence had collapsed. Nevertheless, they continued to adhere to their traditional costumes and ways of life and did not desire or were incapable, at least during the first years of their absorption in Israel, of creating a new set of values and alternative social images.[1]

They were also fanatically religious. The small band of feminist women in Israel could expect little support, strength and solidarity from these oppressed, confused and disorientated women with whom they had little in common. Even their language was different for, not speaking Hebrew, these *Sephardi*[2] women did not even share a common Yiddish heritage.

The leaders were unused to their role and had among them few visionaries and even fewer idealists. The pattern of life had already been set by the Zionist leaders of the Diaspora and there was nothing to counteract the primitive form of Zionism which dominated the thinking of the society. The country was run by paternalists, 'a cult of "the state" was born in 1948, its high priest was Ben Gurion'.[3] Avihai writes:

The point to be borne in mind is that Ben Gurion was in the early stages *the* civil authority. The army was loyal to him and he weeded out (or was willing to release) people near the top who might challenge his unique position. On the other hand, Ben Gurion did obtain cabinet approval for major defense actions, but during most of his service, he did not consult with it until he was quite sure his policy would be accepted.[4]

For women this was a disaster. In no area of public life was their voice heard or listened to. At one point, one woman Member of Knesset, much concerned with the rights of women, was chided for using up so much of her debating time in the Chamber on women's issues. She agreed that this was undesirable as she would like also to identify with other matters. However, when she asked some of her colleagues to assist her and also raise women's issues to leave her more time for other matters, she obtained no support.[5]

The Declaration of Independence had stated that the State of Israel 'will maintain complete social and political equality for all of its citizens regardless of religion, race or sex'. But in 1951 it appears to have been necessary to pass a law confirming this. The Law of Equality of Women stated, 'There will be one law for women and men – every legal action and every judicial provision which discriminates against a woman is void.' This made quite specific the direction in which the society was expected to move. Nevertheless, it begs several questions about the status of women until that time in this so-called egalitarian society and about the reasons for a need for reiteration.

During this period, the early 1950s, when the new State's administration was in full bloom, the main legislation consisting of numerous laws and regulations with regard to both working men and women was passed. However, for some members of Knesset equality of provision was not enough. Still seeing women in passive roles, needing protection and guardianship, Beba Idelson,[6] a Member of Knesset, felt the general labour laws were not adequate to allow women to fulfil the destiny and role with which nature had endowed them – that of wife and mother. She therefore required the enactment of special legislation which would protect women from so-called exploitation. Its main effect was to limit the directions in which women could progress and it failed to provide the means by which husbands and wives could undertake joint responsibility for home and work equally. This law, the Female Labour Law of 1954, which is still in force today, is the central law dealing with the rights of women workers, and permits certain limitations in accepting women for any and every job. It stipulates specifically in its first paragraph that: 'The Minister of Labour is authorised, by regulation, to prohibit or limit the employment of women at any work, at any production process or at any place of work which is liable to particularly harm the health of a woman worker.'[7]

This explicit statement limits the powers of women workers to make their own decisions. It also inhibits a woman's ability to negotiate her own position within the Trade Union Movement, thereby discriminating against her with respect to her rights within the democratic process.

The second paragraph deals with night work for women – an area which has been hotly debated since its inception. It reads:

(a) A woman shall not be put to work at night
(b) Night being a span of six hours between 12 midnight and 6 a.m. and in agriculture between 12 midnight and 5 a.m.

This prohibition was not to apply, however, 'to women working at places where the sick are treated or children and the elderly are taken care of, customs services, meteorological stations, international telephone exchanges, police and prison services, airport and marine services, eating places and hotels, newspapers (except printshops), work connected with caring for livestock,' as well as 'administrative jobs or jobs which require a special degree of personal trustworthiness not involving manual labour' or 'where work conditions and circumstances do not permit the employer to check the time when the work is being done'. In addition, 'any employer may receive permission from the Ministry of Labour to employ women at night in his plant in case of emergency or unexpected pressure, or when the work uses material which is likely to spoil quickly and when a state of national emergency has been declared.' In all cases of employing women at night, the employer 'must provide an adequate place for the women to rest, a warm beverage during recess, transportation facilities to and from work (where no regular public transport is available) as well as a twelve-hour break between one working day and the next'. In addition to all the aforesaid the Minister may allow women to work at night in 'places where three shifts are employed, if, in the Minister's opinion, withholding the permission may harm the possibility of employing women and if the night shift will not be to the detriment of the women's health'. Such a permit is to be given for a limited period of not more than two years.

To protect working women in pregnancy the enactment of various laws served to offer some parity of working arrangements because of the special conditions prevailing. However, little onus was put on the men and it is quite clear that working women and working men were seen as separate and therefore different entities for work purposes.

The law prohibiting night work for women offered an opportunity to employers to discriminate in the hiring of women workers. In factories where shift work was necessary, employers might in many cases refuse to hire women in the light of the law's restrictions, since the men employees might have to accommodate themselves to fit in with these requirements. The extra burden of more frequent night work which could result might be a source of discontent among the men at the plant and therefore a situation the employer would try to avoid. Even though the law makes provision for permits, most employers would prefer not to get involved in the process of applying for special permits and the bother of adhering to special conditions. It is simpler to hire men in the first place. This would be the case even though women themselves might want night-work, both because it is more lucrative and because in many cases it is more convenient to work at night when the father is at home with the children.[7] However, in spite of vehement protestations by Ada Maimon and other feminists in the Knesset the Law was passed. The anomalies were never resolved and are still being hotly debated within the Trade Union Movement and among feminists.

From 1948 onwards, then, women lost what little influence they had had. As the men received more prominence and respect so the women diminished in status. Conditioned to acceptance, they did not commit themselves to achieving equality with men.

Gratitude to their 'liberators' held them back from asserting themselves. The first Knesset of 1949 had eleven women members out of a total of 120. The religious parties had made a pact not to include any women on their list, yet for the previous twenty-five years within those parties a large group of women had been working among the women of the country to improve their conditions; providing all kinds of facilities and acting as an important influence within the religious movement. When these women heard that they were to be excluded from the list of candidates they decided to prepare their own list. They felt that they had the right to express the views of women in the Knesset on domestic issues even if they were to be excluded from such matters as defence, foreign policy, etc. However, they were unsuccessful. In the first Knesset they were unable to obtain a single seat. It was not until the fourth Knesset in 1959 that a woman member of the religious parties was elected.[8]

5. Oriental, Arab and Druse Women

During the late 1940's and early 1950's, Ben Gurion's outlook and emphasis changed. From viewing the Jewish state as a means of immigration and development, he began to regard the state's existence as basic to all else. Defence became an end in itself, for the state's existence was still very much in question. Thus immigration was seen both as an abstract principle for which Jewish statehood was attained and also as a means of strengthening the military (i.e. survival) power of Israel. The overwhelming numerical superiority of the Arabs made immigration not only a central national aim, but 'first of all, a necessity for security'. Similarly, immigrant absorption and, particularly, the successful integration of Jewish immigrants from Arab countries were seen as a part of the total strengthening of Israel.[1]

The immigrant women from the Oriental countries were quite devoid of a consciousness directed towards emancipation and new life styles. They were, in fact, more backward even than their predecessors from the shtetl and were more oppressed, more culturally set than any previous settlers. Figures in 1954 revealed that the majority of Oriental women, both veteran settlers and immigrants (53.2 per cent and 57.8 per cent) had attended no school at all and only 13 per cent of the Oriental new immigrants had completed primary education.[2] These Oriental women clearly would not, in that generation, anyway, be allies for their more established sisters. Lissak writes,

In the first two decades after the establishment of the State (there was) ... a certain kind of segregation between the veteran population and the new immigrants from Muslim countries. True, several formal frameworks such as the school and the army succeeded in reducing the preliminary segregation, but the integration of the new immigrants in the veteran society, which characterised the pre-state period, did not occur in the post independence period.[3]

The integration talked of presumably referred to boys only since there was, as we shall see later, selectivity in recruitment of girls into the army.

In general the immigrants took a long time to adjust to their new society. Although immigration and the 'ingathering of the exiles' was the national obsession, few plans were made to help the immigrants with their adaptation. Their productivity in the moshavim in which they were encouraged to live was far less than that of their European counterparts and their ability to support themselves and increase their standard of living fell short of the average. Dov Weintraub writes:

> The sum total ... of underdevelopment expressed itself, however, in the fact that of 171 villages established between 1948 and 1951 (those which by 1958 should have absorbed and activated the basic seven-year capitalization and production timetable) only 24 – or 14 per cent – actually did so and thereby achieved formal consolidation status.[4]

Where the older pioneers were, in the main, free thinkers, the Oriental Sephardi Jews conformed to an orthodox religious ethic which, because most of their society was uneducated, held a rigid grip on its subjects. Weintraub again,

> ... they all adhered to a traditional way of life – both in general and in Jewish terms – to a world which was static, religious, familistic and strongly value and integration oriented. The fundamental image of those Jewish communities was characterised by their extreme conservatism, whose purpose was to uphold an existing value system, in which the present was conceived of in terms of the past, and the future significant primarily as a projection of the present. Hence the lack of autonomous political and economic values in relation to religious and familistic ones, hence, also a stratification model which is symbolised by family, ethnic, religious and rabbinical criteria, and a vision of a kinship-based community.[5]

Over the centuries, while European influences and cultural values had overlaid the Ashkenazi brand of Judaism, for the Sephardi Jews the faith took on a different character. In the fifteenth century they were expelled from Spain and had then settled mainly in Egypt, Morocco and Iraq, so they became cut off from the mainstream of Jewish thought and development. It was from these Arab countries that the majority of immigrants went to Israel; and they brought with them a religion primitive in its application and unaffected by the natural development of time. With it went a lifestyle juxtaposed with that of their previous Arab hosts. The Sephardi Jews, therefore, brought to Israel a set of values and a lifestyle quite at variance with the ethos of Israel. Certainly they knew nothing of female emancipation. For the men, the normal social contacts which they were able to have outside the home – workmates, leisure activities, union involvement – made their adaptation to the Jewish State easier and less oppressive. For the women, most of whom spent all their time at home, life was narrow and restricted. They were offered no positive help to enable them to catch up nor the means to overcome years of neglect and oppression. Unable to function in a modern state, in a modern way, they very soon foundered and sank under the strain of a new lifestyle. Although the Government provided complicated agricultural schemes and created new villages for them, the men, at whom all this energy was directed, resented suggestions that the women should become part of the work force and the productivity of these new settlements never achieved the levels expected of them. For most of the Sephardi women who came to the country, large families and poverty were to be their fate. The transition from the feudal, backward life which they had lived in other parts of the Middle East to the highly sophisticated society of Israel was poorly worked out by the authorities and badly executed with little concern being taken for them once they arrived. Left almost to their own devices they became mere breeding machines and the butt of planners and politicians.

For the Moslem, Druse[6] and Christian women of Israel the War of Liberation of 1948 did not even hold out the limited expectations which it had to the Jewish women. To some, men and women, it had offered only flight and refugee status; for others, those who had remained behind, it had turned them, overnight, into second-class citizens. They were in a minority in a land they knew well and in which they and their ancestors had lived.

They found themselves with certain rights in this new land, the same as those accorded to everyone else. Everyone had the right to vote, the right to join a trade union, the right to the benefits of maternity and child-welfare facilities, the right to education, and the Government of Israel took into account at a national level some of the needs and wishes of the minority groups. But what happened at national level was far removed from the practicalities of everyday life in the Arab and Druse towns and villages throughout the country. Lucas maintains:

> Official policy was to accord equality of rights to all citizens, Arab and Jewish. But in practice the majority of the Arab population, living near the borders,[7] came under military rule and were subject to restrictions on their freedom of movement under the defence (emergency) regulations of 1945 ... The government continued to view the Arab minority as a potential fifth column, and it was not until the mid-sixties, ten years after violent tension on the borders had subsided, that military rule was relaxed.[8]

Although the Israeli Government granted universal citizenship, the needs of the Arab and Druse were neglected by the Central Government, who found it expedient to assume that each ethnic group took care of its own affairs. A major reform of the time, the Compulsory Education Act of 1949, required school attendance of all children from the ages of five to thirteen inclusive, and of adolescents aged fourteen to seventeen who had not had previous elementary education. The law, however, did not carry with it a compulsory programme of school building and teacher training nor the provision of a budget to carry out a programme of this kind. As a result, education remained poor in those areas which were not funded from outside Israel. In this respect the Arab and Druse communities were particularly vulnerable. Jiryis writes:

> Of all the things that have hindered progress in Arab education the most important has been a shortage of trained teachers. The absence of professional teachers was most sorely felt immediately after the establishment of Israel, when the authorities were forced to appoint dozens of untrained people – during the academic year, 1949–50, 90 per cent of the teachers working in Arab schools were untrained. With the increase in the number of Arab schools, a number of secondary school graduates have been recruited as elementary school teachers. In the twenty-year period between 1949 and 1969, the pro-

portion of professional teachers rose from 10 per cent to 45 per cent, but thus, at the beginning of the 1970–71 academic year, more than half the elementary teachers in Arab schools were still not trained.[9]

Because of the nature of Arab societies at the time only outright encouragement on the part of the Israeli Government could have made universal education for Arab children a reality. While all Arab children within the statutory age limit were required to attend school, it was always possible to find ways of keeping them away.

The villages found it hard to absorb and digest all the advanced laws imposed on them in one fell swoop, and in many instances equality remained merely a cliché. For example, the parents didn't object to having their children attend school and receive free instruction, but when the peak farming season came they would not forego the help of the children causing a marked drop in attendance in the village schools during those weeks.[10]

Clearly education was not seen as a necessity and few checks and balances were made by the authorities on the efficiency of the system.

Jiryis again:

Statistics show that an average of 25 per cent of school-age children either drop out of elementary school or fail to attend at all. The authorities themselves are to blame, in that they do not enforce the compulsory education law. They are lax in taking action against parents who prefer to keep their children at home to help with their work, and they ignore conservatives who refuse to send their daughters to school. Only 44 per cent of school-age Arab girls attend school.[11]

With little liaison between the Jewish and Arab communities, law enforcement was almost impossible. A serious approach to universal education alone would have offered Arab women the possibility of progress towards emancipation. Although the Government made social welfare a major priority the provision of services and facilities was largely dependent on money from Jewish organizations abroad.[12] Since much of this was earmarked for 'Jewish' projects rather than national projects, the minority groups benefited less well. Social services were meagre, allowing little opportunity for progress and development.

But, probably, the most important factor which decided the divisiveness of Israeli female society was the continued and systematic lack of communication and cooperation between Jewish women and their sisters in the minority groups. Lucas writes:

> The Jews for their part were barely aware of the existence of the Arab minority in their midst. The local Arabs entered their consciousness only as a threatening shadow on the countryside. The Jewish population as a whole was ignorant of government policy in relation to the Arab minority and had little knowledge of the disabilities inflicted on the Arabs in the name of security.[13]

Although some Jewish women, certainly those who had brought ideas of emancipation from Europe, were aware of the global nature of the oppression of women, they refused to look at the similarities between themselves and their Arab and Druse sisters. Whatever thoughts of political solidarity among women there may have been, therefore, in the early days of the State and later as the country progressed, these thoughts were never extended to include Arab and Druse women, nor was there a dialogue on the possibilities of such solidarity. Since Arabic was not a compulsory second language in the Jewish schools, communication between Jewish and Arabic women was difficult. Natural relationships and friendships could not spring up since each group was educated separately.

The language and the social, intellectual and economic barriers made contact across cultural lines almost impossible. Where contact did occur, it took the form of condescension and patronage by the Jewish authorities in providing small acts of do-gooding to the Arab communities. Sacher writes:

> The truth was that for nearly twenty years the Israelis, consciously or unconsciously, had sought to isolate their Arab population from the Middle East, and in their first decade of statehood even to isolate the Arabs from Israeli society at large. At no time had the government succeeded in defining any clear, long-term policy towards the Arab minority.[14]

This lack of communication created a situation, inevitably, in which the way Jews and Arabs perceived each other was based on fantasy rather than on any real knowledge. From this, again inevitably, hostilities developed and the Israeli Government retreated from any positive policy of integration. Instead they turned into a virtue the fact that they allowed the Arab communities autonomy, although this in turn reinforced segregation. The status of the Arabs in Israel remained ambiguous. They had the same civil rights as the Jews but were without similar expectations of their citizenship.

As a result little is known of the Arab and Druse women of Israel during the years 1948 to 1967 outside their own societies. In general, they remained within their Christian, Muslim and Druse communities entirely committed to the lives such women had always lived. They were completely dominated by their theocracy, traditions, lifestyles and husbands, remaining chattels, so that the stirrings of the Jewish women hardly affected them. They lived simple, useful lives within the family, retaining strict hierarchical structures. But without social contact, friends from other countries, exposure to other ways, they had almost no opportunity for developing a consciousness of feminism.

Although the Arab villages were surrounded by kibbutzim, the kibbutz women remained rural and secular. There is some evidence of interaction between the two groups in such matters as the passing on of various domestic skills, training in the field of child care, maternity and child welfare, hygiene, etc., although in the main this was carried out for the Arabs by missionaries from abroad. In the more controversial fields of politics, religion and feminism, neither the Jewish women nor the Arab women felt confident enough, nor close enough to share their thoughts or to consider ways of joining together in their mutual oppression.

In terms of social progress, the whole period from the creation of the State in 1948 until the war of 1967 was scarred, gnarled and distorted by the Arab–Jewish conflict. This conflict – between the men of these two races, not the women – impeded any progress towards deeper understanding between the different peoples of the country.

The Arab women were not even able to go into the Army[15] as were their Jewish sisters, and were deprived of the contacts which Army life would have provided. Their physical isolation also cut them off from the mainstream of developing Arab thought. As they were unable to show solidarity with the other groups of women within the country they had no point of strength on which to draw. This was evidenced after the Six-day War when Arabs were once more in contact with their brothers and sisters in neighbouring Arab countries.[16] Sacher writes:

The arrival of those ostensible enemies into Israel was a two-way trauma, for the Israeli Arabs who hosted the visitors no less than for the visitors themselves. The former were reminded of how much they had missed in their quarantine from the surrounding Arab world, deprived of participation in the historic events of Arab nationalism.[17]

The present picture though is not very clear. It is undoubtedly true that some progress towards emancipation has been made and legislative measures enacted by Israel have helped this advancement. Laws providing for the insurance of mothers and for provision of high-level medical facilities has meant that the proportion of women giving birth in hospitals has gone up from 44 per cent in 1949 to 87 per cent in 1974 and infant mortality has dropped from 60 to 38 of every 1,000.[18] In the political arena women are free to vote and to be elected. 'Yet,' writes An'am Zuabi, 'despite the growth of our political consciousness, many women still vote as the men want them to vote, in order to keep peace in the family.'[19] But there is Arab women representation on the Histadrut bodies, the Women Workers' Council and the Labour Councils and for some time an Arab woman served as head of a local council.

Yet, in spite of this and the fact that more Arab women are working in many fields the conflicts within this stringently traditionalistic society continue. There is still no Arab woman in the Knesset and although women appear at times on the list of candidates their place on the ballot remains unrealistic. Great difficulties remain as epitomized by An'am Zuabi, to whom the last word must be given. 'Withal, we are still at the beginning and the path before us is long and difficult. We, the Arab women, must therefore mobilize all our powers in order to achieve the goal we have set ourselves; yet we must not impair the structure of the traditional Arab family.'[20]

6. Dayan, Sinai and the growth of Machismo

As the country developed and the kibbutzim prospered, leading the field in agricultural and industrial organization, women by contrast found themselves undertaking more and more menial tasks. Spiro writes of those times, '... women found themselves in the same jobs from which they were supposed to have been emancipated – cooking, cleaning, laundering, teaching, caring for children, etc. In short, they had not been freed from the "yoke" of domestic responsibility.' And 'An examination of figures of the economic distribution of women in Kiryat Yedidim[1] in 1951 reveals the significant fact that, of 113 physically able women, only 12–14 per cent work permanently in any agricultural branch, while the overwhelming majority – 88 per cent – work in service branches.'[2]

The male population continued to play their initiation games involved with war play and defence strategy and these quickly took over other areas. The lack of conventional discipline and the disrespect for authority and hierarchy in the Armed Forces soon became a national institution. It turned into romantic imagery the brash insolence and arrogance of the troops. Even as early as 1948 the tradition was established by Moshe Dayan himself of whose 'antics' in the 89th Battalion Shabtai Teveth writes:

Moshe's behaviour lent a spirit of devil-may-care audacity to his battalion. Whenever he left the base in his jeep, for example, he would say to his companions, 'Just watch this' and floored the accelerator as they approached the main gate. The jeep would shoot past the startled sentry, who would shout for them to halt. Moshe would bring the jeep to a stop some 30 metres from the gate and arrange his papers for the M.P., who would then have to leave his post and run over to him. His escapades endeared him to his men and he soon became their hero.[2]

Any mode of behaviour, any show of force, any expression of might was condoned and viewed with pride by a nation of backward immigrants, Arabs and by adoring Jewish wives, mothers and sisters. In 1953 the Army carried out a raid on Kibya in Jordan in retaliation for various raids carried out by the Jordanians across the border. During the raid sixty-nine Jordanians, half of them women and children, were killed. Although there were individual expressions of regret over the episode, the matter was hushed up by Ben Gurion, who at no time accepted responsibility for the raid. In 1953, too, 'the peaceful villagers of Kfar Kassem were massacred as they returned home from the field, unknowingly violating a curfew that had been hastily imposed on the eve of the Sinai war. The officers responsible for the killing were indeed court-martialled, but were later amnestied.'[4]

In the 1950s there was a change in emphasis from matters of human and personal progress, growth and development (if indeed these had ever been more than a dream) to one in which the country became dominated and controlled by a power bloc led by the paternalistic David Ben Gurion. Avihai writes:

With the growth in population, Mapai,[5] which had always seen itself as a mass party, continued to attract larger and larger numbers. The intimacy and ideological orientation gave way to a bureaucratic party machine, manipulating ethnic and interest groups and tightly managed by a small central body ... The party became one of mass mobilization, but at its apex an almost incestuous network of family-linked and quasi-family (kibbutz and land settlement leaders) relationships pervaded the structure. Entry into this top echelon was slow and measured. The utopian 'movement-oriented' ideology (or rather spirit-ideology is an overly rational term) combined with a shrewd use of power to control key positions at all levels of government, the Histadrut, labour councils and municipalities. Though the party went through all the democratic procedures of elections from the grass-roots upwards, blocs and alliances within the branches and on the national level gave preferment to 'reliable' members enforcing a relatively strict non-totalitarian democratic centralism which often made the electoral choices from above. The Central Committee, the Secretariat and Politbureau, ostensibly delegated to wield power by the larger elected bodies, became the determining force in party life, which thus took its lead from above. The power of these bodies to

control nominations and appointments was magnified by the pro-
fessionalization of public life, few political figures were independent
financially. They depended on the party for jobs and positions of
power which provided rather modest salaries, but salaries nonetheless,
and that elixir, of the aspiring – a measure of fame, or at least publicity and recognition.[6]

With this shift, the hopes and aspirations of Israeli women
towards equality and egalitarianism faded. The country turned its
back on humanism and pursued a policy of nationalism, militarism and Zionism. Ben Gurion became obsessed with the question of nationalism.

'If the Jewish birthrate is not increased,' he writes in his
memoirs,

it is doubtful that the Jewish state will survive. Any Jewish woman
who, as far as it depends on her, does not bring into the world at least
four healthy children is shirking her duty to the nation, like a soldier
who evades military service. And it is the duty of the Jewish people as
a whole to provide women with the economic, cultural and social
conditions to enable them to give these children a proper upbringing
and education. Every Jewish mother can and must understand that
the unique situation of the Jewish people, not only in Israel but
throughout the world (for the fate of Diaspora Jewry depends to a
large, if not an overwhelming extent on the security and well-being of
the nation of Israel) imposes on her a sacred duty to do her utmost for
the Nation's rapid growth. One of the conditions for growth is that
every family have at least four sons and daughters, the more the
better.[7]

While women continued to serve in the Armed Forces their role
grew less and less important as their lack of status (as a result of
Ben Gurion's decision in the first Knesset) became evident. Writ-
ten descriptions of women soldiers depict their second-class position and their peripheral value. Rolbant writes patronizingly of
them:

Army educators and disciplinarians say the presence of girls in the
camp restrains the men from unruly behaviour and using foul
language, makes a pleasant social atmosphere and boosts the morale
of the fighting men. Here, boys learn how to speak to the opposite sex
under the surveillance of their superiors, and become acquainted with

the special world of women on the threshold of their lives. They dis-cover the values girls treasure most, and what is expected of them in order to gain their confidence and respect. Equally strong is the influence of camp life on the girl. She may listen to lectures that she would normally miss and on subjects that have a direct bearing on what it takes to be a conscientious woman ... An important contribution to her development is provided by her work with officers, with whom she is posted for auxiliary functions. Here is a type of young man whom, but for the army, she would ordinarily be unlikely to meet. Although he is only five or six years her senior she regards him as a teacher and a guide and often visits his family. The relationship is both formal and friendly and he will drop her off on his way home. Years later, when she comes for a month's duty as a reservist, she may find herself working with reserve officers who in private life are economists, school directors or civil servants. She gets a glimpse of life that is varied and many sided, and develops a self-assurance and initiative that prove valuable assets in her future life.[8]

Although conscription is compulsory for both men and women and women are offered the same expectations as men, Bowden writes:

A very high percentage of Israeli males are in fact conscripted. What would be regarded as grounds for exemption in almost any other army – flat feet, colour blindness and illiteracy, do not apply in Israel. Exemption for women ... is much more common. In effect, the IDF only inducts the best educated girls from the high school.[9]

And Joseph Eaton notes, 'When youths reach the age of 18, boys are expected to report for thirty-six months service and girls for twenty-four months. Men remain on reserve duty until the age of 55. Women are generally discharged when they marry, or before, if not needed.'[10]

Ben Gurion's ultra-nationalistic remarks had the effect of negating the woman's role in the army and therefore in society too. As child-breeders and rearers their role in the Army appeared to be to ensure that they met men of superior status with whom they could breed superior sons, thus perpetuating a race of 'holy' soldiers.

In 1953 Moshe Dayan took up his post as Commander in Chief of the Defence Forces, creating in effect a monocracy and his authority remained virtually unchallenged for the next twenty years. With the political emphasis on nationalism the role of the Armed Forces took on greater and greater significance. Generals were assured of high political and civic office and the only way to progress and achievement was via the Army, the Navy or the Air Force. In 1954, Dayan, as Chief of Staff, drew up a plan to facilitate the retirement of Army officers at the age of forty and bribed reluctant 'pensioners' with the top jobs in society. Shabtai Teveth writes,

> Dayan's concept had far-reaching influence on Israeli society. His 'Double-life' plan let loose into civilian life forty-year-old ex-officers – talented, ambitious, vital men at the height of their powers. The economy began wooing these youthful pensioners with offers of top-level positions, so much so that the profile of Israeli society assumed an increasingly military aspect.[11]

As Perlmutter says,

> The military élites have been diffused among the industrial technocrats and bureaucratic élites of Israel. A tacit and highly institutionalised pattern has been established between the Army and society ... officers turnover in Zahal is rapid; the society then absorbs the much needed young officers ... Zahal's graduates are achievement orientated and are pragmatic, experienced managers. The highly nepotistic Histadrut enterprises, the politically appointed senior civil servants, the government-dominated 'private' co-operatives; and the politically orientated kibbutzim all compete for the politically 'neutral' and administration-orientated Zahal officers. Thus a Zahal officer develops an alternative career while still serving in the army.[12]

Victory in the Sinai campaign[13] confirmed the armed forces as the dominant component in the country's economy and lifestyle. As well as being politically significant, the Campaign gave the Israelis an opportunity to flex their muscles, to examine their bravery and to practise their manhood once again. On these counts they were very successful. The battle gave an important stimulus to the significance of the Israeli Armed Forces both inside and outside the country. Luttwak and Horowitz write:

> The campaign gave stature to Israel, showed her to be a determined and reliable partner and demonstrated her military strength.

Regarded until then as little more than a transitory anomaly in an all-Arab region, Israel now became a recognised power within it ... Most important, perhaps, was the renewed confidence inspired by the victory. The post-independence period had been marked by poverty and growing insecurity, many veteran settlers were disillusioned and many newcomers disappointed. 1956 was thus an important psychological turning point.[14]

From their success in battle grew a cult of toughness among the young people which remained with them until the war of 1973. The Sinai campaign organized directly by Moshe Dayan and supported as it was by Britain and France, assured the country an easy victory.[15] The Armed Forces became the saviours of the nation; without them the State would fall apart. Lucas writes:

The new young generation of immigrants achieved a sense of equality with the old-timers by dint of their participation in battle. The legend of 1948 which imparted an aura of exclusiveness to the veterans now faded in the shadow of the brilliant military personality displayed by the modern army of Israel. Military hubris became an integral component of the national personality. The comradeship of battle also assisted social integration. Materialistic pursuits, competitive consumerism buoyed by the rapid economic growth, gradually relegated the pioneering mentality to the tedious gossip of the old. The new national identity began to take firm shape and the 'normalisation' of Jewish life that Zionism had pursued ironically became the epitaph of socialist-Zionism.[16]

Dayan, continuing to dominate and control single-handedly the performance of the Israel Defence Forces, saw the Campaign as his personal game on which he intended to build his national reputation. Teveth writes:

Late on the night of the 30th, he visited Ben Gurion, who had come down with influenza. Here he heard that the Anglo–French force had postponed their attack on the Egyptian air bases by twenty-five hours. Until then, the Egyptian Air Force would be able to operate freely, and Ben Gurion, who was worried about the paratroopers in the Mitla Pass,[17] requested that they be brought back to Israel that night. Dayan cheered him with the confident prediction that even without the Anglo–French invasion Zahal could successfully complete 'Operation Kadesh'. Dayan spared Ben Gurion the unpleasant news of Simhoni's[18] breach of discipline and the premature entry of the 7th

Brigade into battle without a proper operative plan. He apparently did so out of a desire not to provoke Ben Gurion (he told the Prime Minister the details only three days later) but also because secretly he sympathized with commanders like Simhoni, who were so like himself. He commented in his diary, 'Better to be engaged in restraining the noble horse than in prodding the reluctant mule.'[19]

Luttwak and Horowitz exploring Dayan's part in the Sinai campaign write:

As for overall strategic control, this was exercised by Dayan in person. Dayan would fly, drive or otherwise contact the brigade divisional or area headquarters and issue his orders on the spot. Frequently, out of touch with GHQ in the rear, Dayan improvised as he went from place to place, sometimes in radio contact with Tel Aviv and sometimes not. In the absence of systematic control by a central staff it is not surprising that GHQ were sometimes ignored.[20]

Psychologically, the Sinai Campaign was a big setback for the women. Any thoughts of equality were completely destroyed after 1956. The Army's needs were the country's needs and no other philosophy had the slightest chance of survival. Advancement in every field was dependent on performance in the Army. It set the tone of life. The man with the eye patch[21] in all the newspapers symbolized militancy and epitomized machismo. At last, after generations in which Jewish men had been seen, and had seen themselves, as effete and powerless, their successes both in 1948 and cumulatively in 1956 became part of the cultural pattern. Despite the fiasco of the event in political terms they rejoiced in the victory of 'the holy army of Israel'.[22]

The interrelationship between the Army, politics and industry became overt after 1956 and is described by Perlmutter:

Since Sinai, the defence establishment has become the chief client of Israel's technological and scientific achievements. It has invaded the private market as well as large scale modernisation enterprises. Next to the Histadrut and the civil service, it has become Israel's chief employer. Here it threatened the civilian industrialization enterprises of Israel. Criticism came from various directions triggered by the threat of an industrial-military complex: the invasion of military men into the managerial class; the destruction of civilian infant industries; and the danger of the Defence Ministry becoming an autarchy, harnessing industrial developments and the free market, etc. The Ministry argued that autarchy in industry and science for defence purposes was a must in Israel and that it did not threaten established industries but pioneered new industrial industries. The Ministry's aggrandizers prevailed, under the dynamic and mobilizing leadership of Peres,[23] supported by Ben Gurion. Dayan's doctrine that Zahal should not be burdened with the problems of supply and production also enhanced the aggrandizement of the defence 'empire'.[24]

As the country lost its early pioneering spirit, immigration waxed and waned, political differences grew. International recognition as a result of the Suez affair gave the leaders an exalted idea of their importance and took from them the will or the need to consider the nation's wants. Much time was spent wooing the United States into giving money to the country and political and military leaders commuted between Tel Aviv and New York, creating a false image of a mighty nation. The people were grateful; too grateful to their leaders, their generals, their soldiers to make demands, express needs, demand action on the domestic front. As the country moved into the 1960s the euphoria of the 50s turned into complacency. Because of its concentration on military needs and the obsession of its leaders (who included many military men) with World Jewry rather than its own people, the country lost its idealism. Military men in every sphere of life left no scope for the influence of visionaries or innovators. The country was moving from an agricultural, idealistic proletariat looking for inspiration to the collectivist philosophy of the kibbutzim and the idealism of the pioneers, to an undirected, hierarchical, paternalistic bureaucracy, dominated by a military élite. Elon writes:

The paternalism of the veterans grew naturally from their role as a self-proclaimed pioneer élite. Like many former revolutionaries who have grown old in office, they came to believe not only in their own irreplaceability, but in the infallibility of their judgment as well. Veteran Israeli leaders still habitually display an aristocratic contempt for what they disdainfully called the 'masses' or the 'man in the street'. The socialists among them are often more disdainful of 'the street' than the non-socialists, for the early idealism of the former has been corroded by their many years in office. Their political experience has taught them that only organized power matters. They are notoriously insensitive to public opinion that is not formalized as an ideology, as a political party, or as an organized pressure group. Hence the habitual contempt of the ageing mandarins to the results of public opinion polls.[25]

Political infighting left no time for real concern for the people. Power was in the hands of a small group, dominated until 1963 by Ben Gurion. Ruben Slonim writes: 'Israel is dominated by a political machine with power Tammany Hall[26] might well envy. It controls an estimated 250,000 jobs in the country's proliferating bureaucracy and through its monopolistic industries.'[27] Social policy was based, almost entirely, on what the World Jewish Congress and the United Jewish Appeal would supply money for. Brecher writes:

(Yet) America remained vital in Israel's foreign policy. It had sponsored the Johnston Plan[28] for the Jordan Water in 1953–5. It pursued an ambivalent policy during the Sinai Campaign which proved to be crucial – pressure for Israeli withdrawal and a pledge for safeguards against a recurrence of Egyptian security threats. It continued to extend aid in multiple forms; direct grants and loans (more than a billion dollars in 1968); permission to American Jewry to make donations as partially tax-exempt charity ($1½ billion before the 1967 war and a further $250 million during that crisis); preliminary co-operation for a future desalination project, the key to irrigation of the Negev Desert;[29] and technical assistance for special needs.[30]

But little of this money found its way into projects aimed directly at helping the more underdeveloped sectors of the community. While the Sephardi immigrants, hindered by large families which were offered little direct Government help, failed to achieve a position in society, the Ashkenazi group with their skills, expertise and contacts moved the country forward towards a truncated form of Western bourgeois culture. As this bourgeoisie grew, through its powerful male manipulation of all areas of power and influence, any concerted will to maintain principles disappeared, and the nation gave way to the cult of militarism, violence and male dominance.

The women, excluded as they were from the battle for supremacy, reverted slowly to the only role they were sure of – that of wife and mother. Writing of Gadna, the pre-military cadet corps,

Eaton states: 'The co-educational make-up of Gadna prepares women for such supportive roles and reinforces the idea that national demise affects everybody. As future mothers, girls should know what will be required of their husbands and sons.'[31]

With the growth of male supremacy, motherhood began to take on a new significance, providing as it did a vehicle for glory in the production of sons. Sons who would carry on the tradition of soldier, fighter, victor. Rolbant writes:

> In Israel the child sees his father putting on his uniform to go to the Army for a day every month, and for a whole month every year. His older brother or sister will either be in the regular army at the age of eighteen or else do reserve service. If he lives in one of the new development towns or villages his teacher is a soldier girl doing her military service at the school while others, members of the military agricultural corps, do part of their service as club instructors, youth leaders or cultural workers. The army does not therefore appear as an invasion into civilian life, something outside it and opposed to it, but as a integral part of the child's growth and development.[32]

Excuses, such as Ben Gurion's, for keeping women in their place were easily found, for who else could produce the babies the country so desperately needed? In a country such as Israel these manipulative arguments easily defeated the women, conditioned as they were by generations of paternalism and theocracy.

Within industry, the civil service and politics, positions of power were handed out not because of merit but as prizes, and these prizes went, almost without exception, to ex-generals and men who had done well in the Armed Forces. Most of these men had little experience of the responsibilities of civilian life or of modern techniques in industry. The narrow concept of society thus created, plus the systematic policy and reinforcement of the superiority of young males, dominated the lifestyle and, semi-consciously perhaps, demoralized the idealists, boorishly and arrogantly denying their existence. Israel in the 1960s was a country without vision. Among Jews in the West its myths sustained it. Totally self-absorbed and prepared to offer a narrow nationalistic view of itself to the outside world, it began to asume an artificial character. Lucas notes:

The new Israeli nation which was established in the nineteen years between the declaration of its independence and the crisis of May 1967 had borrowed heavily on both Jewry abroad and on the Arabs of Palestine to secure its own identity. The elimination of the Palestinian identity was a corollary of the Zionist rationale by which the relation of the state to western Jewry was sustained ... The promotion of a bi-national theory of independence would have swept away the basis of foreign Jewish support. The Zionist underpinning of the Jewish state thus required Israel to dictate to the surrounding Arabs the structure of their own national life.[33]

With a culture based on male dominance and a narrow inward-looking, self-satisfied philosophy there was little space for ideals of female equality.

By 1966 the country was in an economic depression. The peace on the borders started to crumble as the Arabs in neighbouring countries began to assert themselves. To maintain its superiority and to lull the population, the Army began to carry out intermittent raids into bordering Arab States. Lucas writes:

The economic recession which began in 1965 had assumed crisis proportions by the end of 1966. There were few signs of improvement in the spring of 1967. Emigration increased and morale was low ... The public had begun to lack confidence in the government. A political crisis thus compounded the economic and military stress, and a general gloom descended to displace the verve that had come to typify public life.[34]

The Armed Forces maintained their position as the sacred cow. Nothing could shake the faith of the people in their supremacy. In public, no one voiced moral or ideological opposition. Children grew up believing and accepting without question the inevitability of Army service. This was the school-leaving certificate. Admission to the army was a man's recognition of his potency. Rejection meant failure and disapproval for life. Rolbant writes:

... you cannot intellectually refuse military service unless you deny Israel's right to exist; conversely, joining the Army is a natural concomitant of state membership. That is why new immigrants, or people uncertain of their membership of Iraeli society, or who feel that they have not been admitted as equals into it, are so keen on joining the Army. Nothing so much as membership in the Army emphasizes the fact that they are like everybody else. By putting on his uniform the new soldier wishes to remind his environment that he is not a Moroccan Jew but a rightful and recognized member of his society ... One's whole life – education, travel, marriage, housing, etc. – is somehow touched by years of army service which incisively integrates into the general framework of life.[35]

For the men, fear and the glory of death in battle were natural obsessions. Writing of the exploits of Gadna (regiments of youth) Elon notes:

Gadna operates in conjuction with the educational authorites in nearly all of the high schools. Senseless tests of endurance under excrutiatingly difficult conditions of climate and terrain in the name of a spartan ideal of physical fitness have led to fatal accidents among teenagers. Almost every summer a number of children die of sunstroke in the desert where they have been made to march for days, or stumble down deep precipices while walking on narrow mountain paths in exercises designed to steel their nerves and train them for unflinching courage.[36]

For the women, widowhood was an honour and the production of sons for the country was glorious. The deep need of Jewish women to honour the penis, a need that had existed throughout history in one form or another, became the accepted way of life for Israel. And among the establishment this was fully accepted. The paternalism of the leaders who, according to Elon 'prescribe to mothers the number of babies they ought to have,' silenced protest, particularly from women. They remained subservient and passive, fearful of endangering the survival of the State if they had not found the identity they had sought in early times, and amazingly they appeared content with their situation.

7. The Six-Day War and the Influence of the United States

1967 – and the June war of that year was for Israeli manhood the jewel in its crown of military achievement. 'It was Israel's golden summer,' wrote Abba Eban. At first, stunned by the scale of their success and dulled by what they saw as the huge potential of their small citizens' fighting army (an army from which Arabs, Druse, and women – Jewish, Arab and Druse women – were excluded) they were ecstatic. Not only had they enlarged their borders; reunified Jerusalem, reached the Suez Canal; they had also re-valued themselves in their own eyes and in the eyes of the whole world. Abba Eban wrote:

Hereafter, Israel would project a new vision of itself to its own people and to the world beyond. It had given proof of resilience and determination; it had shown the qualities that glow most brightly in adversity; and it had carried its banner forward in an atmosphere of intense world sympathy. Wherever Jews walked in the streets any-where in the world, there was a new confidence in their step. Israel, after all, was not a Great Power. It would always be small in size and material strength. Surely, then, its victory bore witness to special qualities of spirit ... A sense of spiritual vigour went out from its shores and set imaginations astir in many lands.[1]

Without too much regard for the vast and serious long-term consequences, the Six-Day War had been, for the Israeli Defence Forces, the proving ground which had confirmed, not only among the armed forces of the world, but among their own people, their superiority as a fighting force in world terms. The 'manhood' of the State had been on trial and had proved itself to be as potent as it had hoped it was. During the months leading to the War, during all the Egyptian harassment, the world, looking on, had not expected such achievement from Israel. Israel, too, was not quite sure of herself and was fearful of the consequences of fighting such a tough hostile army. Herzog writes:

On the morning of 5 June Israel struck – and within six days had destroyed a great part of the force which had threatened it, occupying the Sinai Peninsula, the Gaza Strip, the West Bank of the Jordan and the Golan Heights. This transformation from a potentially helpless victim into a brilliant victor created a euphoria which brought about a revolutionary change of attitude in Israel. Against the background of sombre prospects a few days before, their incredible victory evoked a reaction throughout the Jewish world such as Israel had never known or experienced.[2]

While the cult of manhood and the mystique of violence had been growing steadily through the years after independence, the 1967 war confirmed and reinforced the acceptance of the dogma of the Army. It was invincible, awesome and idealized. Apprenticeship for Israeli life was served by men in the Army and the accomplishment of the Six-Day War completed this apprenticeship. And this 'great' Army – the brain-child of Moshe Dayan, created before the Suez Campaign which acted as a testing ground for it, ignored the existence of women. They took no part in the fighting force and therefore no part in the glory. They remained servile. Mention of them in the literature is demeaning and humiliating. Rolbant writes:

The induction of women at the age of eighteen for twenty months has an important budgetary aspect. Without it the Army would have to hire thousands of civilian personnel to act as telephone operators, signallers, typists and clerical workers. However, there is also a very important moral consideration to justify their recruitment ... Even parents who have no boys get the feeling that they are equally responsible for the defense of the country.[3]

But they had some part to play, for the era of the bereaved mother, the war-widow, the orphaned children, had arrived. Their stoicism, passivity, conformity were an example to the country. The Army in its wisdom took over as father figure. War-widows and bereft children became the responsibility of the Army. Generals were seen, and photographed, attending *Barmitzvot*, weddings and university graduation ceremonies of orphaned children.

Wives of dead soldiers had a duty to turn to the Army for advice, help, financial support, counselling. Not only had they suffered great loss but the Army placed a duty on them to be grateful. Commanding officers were not only experts in warfare, they were paterfamilias to boot.

As the war receded and the self-conceit became part of the way of life, the euphoria continued. These self-styled deliverers of the nation became a familiar sight, strutting and swaggering their way around the country as the State began its new existence within its enlarged borders. As these borders and the re-integration of Jerusalem unfolded their potential for change, Israel began to feel and demonstrate its new power. During the June war the involvement of American Jewry had been grandiose and fairly unexpected. Funds poured in from the Israel Emergency Fund set up by the World Jewish Appeal. Many United States organizations halted their usual fund-raising activities to concentrate on the bigger issue of Israel. One luncheon alone netted $15,000,000 in fifteen minutes as individuals raised bank loans and cashed life insurances to raise money. The International Ladies Garment Workers Union purchased one million Israel bonds and Mt Sinai Hospital in New York agreed to pay the salaries of doctors who went to serve in Israel. When the war was over the figure raised was in the region of $180,000,000 before the campaign closed. With this kinds of response coupled with the magnitude of the victory, American Jewry was ripe for exploitation. Moshe Davis writes:

> The Six-Day War inspired the whole people, and religious Jews saw the hand of Providence at work. In those heady days, the issues were clear, the victory astounding and the return to Jerusalem certainly lifted events out of the stream of ordinary everyday history. Secularists who could not bring themselves to speak of 'Miracles' except metaphorically, at least testified to the uniqueness of the events of 1967.[4]

As a result of American Jewry's patronage the country prospered. There was a mood of reconstruction and development. New jobs were created in all fields to anticipate and encourage this as the country, after a long period of unemployment, low morale, depression and lack of economic growth, found itself once again important in the eyes of world Jewry. Jews from all over the world flocked to the country to see this new phenomenon – the powerful, victorious, Israeli-Jewish male. The new jobs, high in prestige, status and influence were given out to army personnel of the Officer Corps who, now the war was over, were looking for ways of maintaining their over-inflated egos. (The Israeli Army does not maintain a large regular force.) The country became one large, male club whose initiation ceremonies were concerned with military prowess. The praise and adulation Israel received at that time made it feel strong enough to claim its potential as a real home for the Jews of the world. It felt strong, powerful and was, of course much larger and more economically viable, offering greater opportunities for investment from abroad. Lucas writes:

> The disastrous policy of the occupation, which squandered the fruits of the military victory of 1967 and made Israel less secure than at any time in its history, was not only uncritically accepted by foreign Jewries but had become the very source of their enthusiasm. The occupation itself had in fact become the security problem of Israel. And yet the Israeli government could never have counted on comparable Jewish support for a policy, say, of integrating the Arab minority fully within the national life of the country. It was Israel as conqueror that evoked the most generous support, launching the country after 1967 on its most buoyant economic expansion yet.[5]

Money poured in from the United States and was received sycophantically. Amos Elon describes the times:

> ... the country never seemed more self-confident than in the years after 1967, never in such a steady upsurge in so many fields of civilian life. Industry and building boomed, the rate of investment grew; education, tourism, the social services, even the arts expanded as never before. More books were written and sold. The number of art galleries rose by a third. Never had there been as many night clubs, fancy restaurants, fashionable boutiques, cosmetic salons, *boites* and discotheques for teenagers. In Tel Aviv alone, there were almost twice as many theatres in 1969 as there had been three years earlier. An ambitious programme was launched in Tel Aviv for slum clearance, urban renewal and beachfront development. A new university, the seventh in the country, was opened in Beersheba,[6] two more were planned for the near future ...

The country's rate of economic growth soared from 1 per cent in 1967 to 13 per cent in 1968 and 9 per cent in 1970. More and more immigrants were arriving in the country from affluent and 'safe' countries. Between 1947 and 1967, 15,000 United States immigrants had arrived. In the June war another 10,000 entered the country, half of whom remained. From then until 1973 immigration from the North American continent averaged 5,000 a year increasing the total number of Americans and Canadians in the country to 40,000 by 1973.[7]

The most important factor in this immigration trend was the reunification of Jerusalem. The whole concept of this city, now made whole again, the symbolism of the freedom of religious worship at the Western Wall,[8] caught the imagination of the Jews of the West. The government was quick to exploit this and used the idea to develop her policy of immigration, obtaining large sums of money to finance it and diverting badly needed person-power to administer it. The Jewish Agency was enlarged and more and more envoys were sent out to all the large cities in the United States and Western Europe to encourage Jewish families to settle in the State of Israel. Needless to say this highly emotion-laden policy was aimed at encouraging the men of the family, the built-in assumption being that the women and children would follow. It is well known that single and divorced women were not encouraged and sometimes actively discouraged from emigrating.[9]

8. The Era of the Russian Immigrant

Golda Meir's career as Prime Minister from 1969 to 1973 did nothing to alter the male-domination of the country. Indeed her premiership served only to foster it. As one of the few members of the higher echelons of power who had not been directly involved with the War, she relied heavily on her all-male cabinet to direct her thinking in areas concerned with defence and intelligence. As she was totally besotted by the male mystique which gripped the country, she did nothing to open the eyes of the society to the wasted potential of the women who were part of that society. She was completely involved with presenting herself as both a powerful leader and as a warm, humane, feminine figure, 'the sentimental, intuitive, extroverted, Mrs Meir', writes Michael Brecher. She it was who encouraged, to an alarming extent, the immigration from the Soviet Union, without preparing the climate and the social and economic conditions at home to absorb it; nor was she concerned for the diplomatic issues involved. Frequently she was seen at Lod Airport, tear-stained and embracing, as plane loads of confused Russian Jews flew in. Her presence was the equivalent of a Good Housekeeping Seal of Approval. Sacher notes:

... two years later (1969) Mrs Meir informed the Knesset that her government henceforth would continue to press for the free emigration of all Soviet Jews who wished to depart for Israel. She kept her word. From then on, lashing back at Soviet policy with every resource of public disclosure, the Meir cabinet helped orchestrate the campaign on behalf of Russian Jewry, utilizing American Jewish organizations, international committees of scientists, musicians and other professionals, appealing to the United Nations, to political and even Communist leaders in other lands. Special prayer services for Soviet Jewry were conducted at the Western Wall. Highly publicized demonstrations and vigils were mounted outside Soviet embassies in Washington and other western capitals. No channel of communication was neglected to arouse public opinion in the free world. Nor was there ever doubt that Israel's purpose in this campaign was less to improve the status of Soviet Jews than to revive their Jewish identity, kindle their hopes of emigration to Israel, and ultimately to acquire their presence and talents for the growth of the Jewish state.[1]

Totally absorbed in this activity, events at home completely passed her by. But worst of all she offered no lead to her country's women for self-actualization and no positive acknowledgement of their existence. No reform valuable to women was accomplished by her efforts. Instead she colluded with the current cult and refused to identify with the real issues facing the country – issues concerned with the problems of present-day morality, equality and national justice. For Golda's militaristic policy was narrowly based on two fronts – that of immigration and a form of Zionism. To any of the other more personal, deeply held views of members of her society, her response was cavalier and nauseatingly grandmotherly. Simha Dinitz, the Head of her Bureau at the Foreign Office from 1963 to 1965 recalled, when she became Prime Minister, 'Since she is a Jewish mother and Jewish grandmother, she superimposes family feeling on national destiny.'[2]

As a result money and valuable time were wasted. Time which could have been spent on important radical reform within the country, strengthening it and helping it face the future, was lost. Lacking experience and expertise, the Meir Government soon became politically out of its depth. Spurred on by a belief in the myth of its own military infallibility the Government systematically squandered its greatest military asset, the flexibility of the offensive capacity of its troops, by adopting a policy of occupation geared to the rigid defence of distant foreign territories. After 1967 Israel developed an imperial persona corresponding with the Arab stereotype of it. Instead, then, of the valuable feminist influences of the late 1960s being felt in Israel, as they were in the United States, Great Britain and France, the image of the 'earth mother' took hold, the perfect foil to the busy activity needed to maintain the already inflated male ego.

The 'earth mother' image had little to counteract it. Birth control, always available to the rich, middle-class Ashkenazi women of the country, was not universally accepted. This meant that the poorer communities and the Arab and Druse women who had little knowledge of the subject and poor access to facilities, continued to have large families which they neither wanted nor could afford. 'From 1951–66,' Ben Gurion writes, 'the Jewish birthrate declined from 26.1 to 16.1 per thousand, whereas among the Arabs it rose from 37.6 to 43.4.'[3] It meant, too, that the fecundity of Arab women (no different in reality from that of any other group of women) could be used in the immigration argument, as a large Jewish population would counteract what was seen to be an abnormally large growth in the Arab population of the country. Since abortion was illegal and other forms of contraceptive advice non-existent, women had no means of limiting their birthrate from choice. Had a sensible policy been introduced, the persecutory feeling that the Arabs of Israel were conspiring to choke the Jewish people by over-population might have been stemmed. Such 'new' ways of thinking may have been one step in the direction of liberation of women in that they would have the right to control of their own bodies, thereby taking the personal and private question of birth and motherhood out of the political arena altogether.

In this field the Social Welfare agencies were of little value. In the division of Ministries by political parties – a traditional means of political organization – the religious parties had been given the administration of the Social Welfare Ministry. Their policy was strictly against birth control and abortion, and social workers could find themselves without a job if they were to recommend either to their over-burdened, oppressed clients.[4]

The Meir Government, because of the success it had in the United States and because it was looked on benignly by the rest of the West, had in its power the ability to transform the political and social ethos of Israel. This opportunity was never seized and the country was to experience a process of degeneration from which it will have great difficulty recovering.

Golda Meir, because of her popularity abroad, her ability to raise money in the United States and her position in the country as one of its oldest pioneers, managed successfully to inhibit any stirrings towards female expressions of their rights. At no time did Golda identify with the oppressed women of her race and showed no sympathy for them. In her policy of immigration and reaffirmation of the Zionist philosophy, the traditional Jewish female stereotype was of fundamental importance.

By 1971, after Golda Meir had been Prime Minister for two years, the oppression of women had become so institutionalized that it was no longer apparent. Women carried their mantle of suffering without even being aware of it. They were grateful for everything; for the Great Israeli Army which had offered them protection and which blatantly paraded its acceptance of its role of protector; grateful to Meir for what was seen as her ability as a woman to lead the country; grateful to the United States; grateful to the tourists; grateful for the false policy of immigration which poured money into a cause from which there was little positive value and which kept them and their children poor and under-privileged. There was little discontent. The guilt which the poor, oppressed women of Israel had for feelings that were anything less than passive, paralysed them into stagnation.

In those first years of Golda Meir's leadership, nobody questioned the lack of legislation to improve the lot of women; the inequality of wages and salaries; the dearth of career opportunities; in a society where almost every job of note and every position of power and influence in the fields of politics, social welfare, immigration, business, industry, trade unionism, education, health, was given to men.

9. Boom Years 1971 to 1973

In spite of the poor political situation and general moral decline the years 1971 to 1973 were boom years for Israel. Since 1967 money had been pouring in from the United States. There seemed no end to the generosity of the American Jews. In order to maintain this cornucopia Israeli leaders spent most of their time flying back and forth to the United States reinforcing the image of Israel, trying to appeal to the sympathies of American Jewry. Golda, on visits, would ensure that she went to Milwaukee, the town from which she had originally emigrated to Israel, sentimentalizing and publicizing her connections with that city. Israel, also, was constantly playing host to groups of American fund raisers who could be seen and were photographed touring the country in buses, visiting army bases and being sycophantically received by Jewish Agency functionaries. For all, these visits to Army field units were obligatory so that the soldiers could be admired and battle-stories told and re-told. The response of these visitors was uncritical and idolatrous. Sacher writes:

> Since the 1967 victory, generals had become Israel's new heroes, and the objects increasingly of an emergent personality cult. The focus of unrestrained adulation, they became natural vote-catchers for political parties. Indeed, those who resigned from the armed forces often moved directly into political life with virtually no interim apprenticeship.[1]

This exaggerated form of flattery went to the heads of the men as nothing else did. The Army, above reproach, subject only to the beneficence of the Jews of the Diaspora, became slovenly, boastful, braggardly and obnoxious as they swaggered and swanked their way through the society – the most chosen of the chosen people. Sacher notes:

> The moral sclerosis that afflicted Israeli life following the 1967 war

did not spare the army. Flattered, wined and dined, generals began taking liberties with their rank, eating at the best restaurants on the defense ministry's expense account, cultivating newly expensive tastes in clothes, and automobiles, allowing their soldier-chauffeurs to serve their families.[2]

As the shoals of 'distinguished' Israelis jetted their way across the Atlantic to scrounge in whatever way they could from the Americans, they were left with little time or interest to concern themselves with the quality of life of the Israeli people. The philosophy of the country was that survival equalled money, there could not be one without the other – American money was the survival of the country. Security, development of the territories and immigration were the issues, and those could as well be discussed in Washington, Paris, Vienna, London, even in the Vatican, as in Tel Aviv, Haifa, Ashdod or Petach Tikva. There was so much personal kudos to be achieved and no criticism to deflate the ego.

The great policy of immigration, intended systematically to increase the Jewish population, only succeeded in trying to replace those Israelis who were leaving the country in droves. By 1975, 300,000 Israelis had settled in the United States alone.

As the degeneracy quickened, the Government refused to be side-tracked from its obsessive pursuit of the American dollar. Issues at home were ignored. No efforts were made nor ideologies proffered to counteract this dependency on the United States, neither to make Israel more self-sufficient and independent nor to think about progressive plans for the future. In order to run the country in the way she wanted and to remain in office Golda Meir needed to ensure that the coalition was united. It was essential for her to keep the relationship between the alignment and the National Religious Party harmonious. To this end she intended to ensure that the religious parties were not faced with issues which were offensive to them. Such issues would be those concerned with domestic affairs; questions relating to Civil Marriage, abortion, etc. It was in her interests to submerge these matters and concentrate on those which were more highly emotive and which helped to maintain the myth of imminent disaster while maintaining that the Army was invincible. No people could have been in a greater dilemma. Arian writes:

As everyone knows, the Israeli army has always been considered almost a perennial miracle-worker, as the one institution that always delivers the goods quickly and almost painlessly, all the while being a natural reserve of fortitude, dedication, honesty and well-nigh puritanism in a modern dynamic society . . . The army was considered for a number of illogical reasons, an island in itself, completely insulated from the harmful and unpleasant symptoms of a competitive, materialistic society.[3]

The politics of the Meir Government were disastrous. Obsessed by the spectre of war, and her fears of conflagration, Golda was paralysed into inactivity in home affairs while frantically shopping around for arms and weapons to fight an enemy which she failed to understand and with which she lacked the political and diplomatic acumen to negotiate. As a result, the rumblings of discontent by various sections of the society, which were beginning in the early seventies, were at best appeased and at worst ignored. A group of Oriental Jews calling itself the Black Panthers (inspired no doubt by the organization of the same name in the United States) formed to protest at what it saw as injustice in housing, employment, education, etc. An organization of young married couples began to protest at housing policies which allocated highly subsidized housing to new immigrants and left them homeless. Anger and unrest quickly followed as a result of enormous tax concessions, given as an incentive to prospective immigrants, which were in strong contrast to the swingeing taxes, both on wages and on consumer goods, paid by the indigenous population.

In spite of the boom, the gap between rich and poor grew wider as year after year the 'easy' money from the United States was squandered on lining individual pockets, avarice and aquisitiveness. 'In short,' writes Sacher, 'materialism and self-indulgence had become the mood of the 1960s and 1970s.'[4]

Elections were scheduled for October 1973 and the country moved towards them in an atmosphere of self-satisfaction and smugness, in spite of the underlying discontent. The barometer was set fair for another term of immoral, paternalistic government. But before this could happen 'the world', as Arian writes, 'changed'. On 6 October 1973, Yom Kippur, 5734, the war began.[5]

10. Women in the Yom Kippur War

The war of 1973 came as a bolt from the blue and had a phenomenal effect on women. The speed of the engagement suddenly removed all the men of fighting age and left those remaining at home shocked and numbed. During the first day or two they needed to make the sudden and dramatic adjustment of putting themselves on a war footing. Emptying the air-raid shelter of domestic junk and making it habitable; getting the kids settled into a calm frame of mind; stocking up with a little food; making windows blast-free and blacked out; they were quickly and heavily occupied. This done, they began slowly to realize, as they came out into the streets, that they were alone in the towns and villages; that only women and men valueless to the Army remained. These men, left at home, felt castrated, impotent, powerless. For the women, feelings were even more destructive. They felt purposeless in their own land, where being purposeful was the only reason for living. There was nothing for them to do and as the war went on they continued having nothing to do.

As the War started, so the country stopped functioning. This meant that, away from the war zones, among the civilian population (mainly women), days were spent in total idleness. Traditionally, all the centres of power and commerce at every level were in the hands of men. The women, therefore, left at home, used only to taking orders, having no economic responsibilities, no areas of control and never used to taking initiatives, had no work. Untrained and unskilled, they were unable to deputize for the men and run the country efficiently.

When most of the men in the labour force were mobilized and taken away from their work, it seemed the economy would come to a halt. The women felt frustrated because they had not been trained, therefore could not replace the mobilized men at the machines, in manufacturing, behind the truckers wheel and in agriculture.[1]

As the truth of their position in society dawned on them the women felt humiliated, debased, ignored. Over the previous year or two, some of them had begun, through the newly formed Women's Movement, to find a voice and to grow in strength and confidence. When the war came, all this stopped. They were useless and had been well and truly put in their place. In a country of only three and a half million people, more than half had nothing to do. Every effort women made to integrate themselves into the war society was thwarted. They asked to be allowed to do jobs usually done by men. Jobs such as truck driving to deliver food supplies – to keep communications open. They were told, 'Yes, such drivers are needed – but only men.' They wanted to set up crèches and centres to take messages from men at the front so that women with valuable skills would be freed from sitting at home waiting for news and could work in the society. They were denied this. The Women's Movement discontinued its activity, the election campaign stopped. A few social workers, nurses, and women doctors were used in the towns to deal with civilian problems. No women, even if their skills were greater than those of the men, were allowed at the Front. Women doctors with skills more relevant to the needs of the wounded were left to look after the domestic clinics in the towns. Male gynaecologists were sent to the Front rather than women anaesthetists, plastic surgeons, orthopaedists. Male paediatricians attended the wounded at Suez and on the Golan Heights, while women physicians and surgeons skilled in treating burns, amputations, shock, etc., were left in Tel Aviv, Beersheva, Jerusalem, Haifa and Safed.

During the Second World War, women were called upon to join the Hebrew ATS (Army Territorial Service). Recruited in a campaign launched by the Jewish community in Palestine, they were required for the war effort in industry and for participation in the armed forces. Women were prominent in the food industry which worked at a high level to provide for the Army. Although in construction they did not do actual building work, women were active as engineers, draughtsmen and in auxiliary tasks. Numerous young women volunteered to drive heavy lorries in the British Army and they could be seen everywhere on the roads, throughout the country and in the Western desert, transporting supplies and ammunition to the allied forces. Some of these women in uniform completed high-level administrative and supply-training courses and later managed giant supply depots and large mess halls, feeding many hundreds of soldiers. As well as this, the Women Workers Council organized special courses to meet the needs of the economy, while the men were away. These ranged from the operation and maintenance of farm tractors to keep the kibbutzim running, and to courses on such things as goat-raising and wool processing, providing raw materials and warm clothes for the population.

In the 1973 war, some of these women, who had then been in their twenties, were still of an age to be useful and valuable to the war effort. None of them were called or used. In the towns, on the kibbutzim, in the villages, life stopped. The women, with nothing to do but listen to the news and wait to hear the fate of their husbands, brothers, lovers, sat and waited to become widows, brotherless, bereft of lovers. A sense of frustration, despair and hopelessness absorbed them. They were totally demoralized. What purpose did they serve? Were the soldiers fighting for them and if so, what concept of them did these soldiers have? Was the thought of the clinging vines left at home shivering and quaking incentive enough to make the fighting worthwhile? Was their reward for injury, maiming and death a subservient female class forever grateful, forever cringing in the shadow of the superman? For each superman must there be a menial woman? Is there no sense of self for the superman without a sense of non-self for the woman? 'Tell my mother I fought like a hero,' said one radio operator minutes before his death at Suez in 1973.[2]

Even the women who were in the Army took no part. As the Syrians rolled their tanks across the Golan Heights, the Israeli Army rolled its women down from the Front to the safety of the towns. The Army did not feel this sudden loss of personnel. The women of the Army had never been trained to take part seriously in combat at any level. They had played no important part, and therefore they were not missed. They felt cheated, conned, deceived into thinking the country's cause was their cause. They were soon to learn this was a game for boys only.

When their initial efforts to become involved with the war failed, the women were left floundering. The men were fighting for them and for their country, but for what kind of country? What kind of future? Self-determination and the struggle to achieve it seemed even harder than before. Independence was not going to be easily won. But as they waited for the 'heroes' to return home; as they prepared to feed them, fuss them, fuck them for the sake of the nation (whatever that was!): as they prepared to listen to the interminable stories of bravery, courage, boldness, self-sacrifice; as they got ready for the medal ceremonies, the pompous burials of the dead, the eulogies, adulation, hero-worship, they had time, for the want of anything better to do, to consider their position, to feel bitter and to be resentful. Smarting and sore they faced the oncoming peace with trepidation.

As the full extent of the fighting and the casualties became known the women began to count their dead and to number their maimed and seriously injured. 'The nation', Sacher writes, 'had lost 2,552 dead and over 3,000 wounded in the eighteen days of fighting, with a high proportion of officers among the casualties.[3] The country, too, began to count the cost. This had not been a war as it had been in June 1967. This time the fighting had been bloody and the casualties great. Young men who had grown up with the myth of the 1967 war and the bravado engendered by it found themselves ill-prepared for the bloodshed, destruction and near-defeat. They were demoralized, contrite and deflated. Although the fighting lasted only three weeks, the male population of the country was tied up on both fronts, Suez and the Golan Heights for three months. In that time, the economy took a dive from which it has still not recovered.

As for the economic costs, these were only beginning to be felt. The expenditure of equipment and damaged property alone reached $4 billion. If one added to this the decline in production and exports as a result of manpower mobilization, the cost soared to $7 million – the equivalent of Israel's GNP for the entire year.[4]

Unprepared, untrained and unknowing, the women had not

been able to take over in a time of great need, nor did society expect that they should. Used to inferior positions in every walk of life, they were not equipped to assume control. The society itself had always been asleep to the potential of its womenpower. Can a country of about three and a half million people really afford to ignore half the population? With full involvement of all its people, men and women of whichever ethnic group, taking an equal part in every aspect of the society's problems the outcome of many may well be different. Efficiency may improve. Attitudes may change and the realization of the total commitment of men and women to each other may take place. As it was, in the 1973 war the men returned to lick their wounds; the women were left to face their own failure.

The Army must take full credit for most of this alienation. For years the myth of equality between men and women in Army life had never been examined. The reality had been easily masked from a populace conditioned from childhood to believe the myth. The facts, however, tell a different story and put a new perspective on the difference of commitment of the two sexes. Israel is the only country where women's service in the army is compulsory. This, apparently, offers some evidence of the rights and duties of all the population of the country. However, the female soldier serves less than two years in the army, in comparison to the boys, who serve three years, and she is automatically discharged when getting married or pregnant. A woman who declares she is religious has more opportunity of deferment than boys. Standards of education for admission to the Army differ between boys and girls. Poorly educated girls are not wanted by the Army whereas equally illiterate boys are drafted and used in various jobs, such as catering, dish-washing, etc. Because of the shorter periods of service, more interesting jobs are closed to women as the policy of the Army is not to invest too much in their training. The Israeli Army has a principle of not endangering the lives of female soldiers – a principle also accepted by the United States Army. There the similarity between the two forces starts and ends.

In the American Air Force, seven out of 109 jobs are closed to women. There are female pilots and test pilots, although they do not serve in fighters. In the Navy, only fifteen out of 102 jobs are closed to women and the picture is similar in other sections of the Armed Forces. In the Israeli Armed Forces, more than half the jobs are closed to women and out of 145 jobs open to them, between fifty and sixty are of an administrative nature, being either secretarial or clerical. However, there is a trend to widen the range of jobs open to women, but these are mainly among the domestic troops and in technical branches.

The term 'women's troop' doesn't exist any more in the U.S.A. Women are integrated in various corps in the Army. In Zahal women are trained separately and belong to the women's corps. In theory women can reach any senior rank in the military profession. In reality she never does. One explanation for this is that women tend not to dedicate as much time as men to military work. A second and complementary explanation is that when there is no equality of duties there is generally no equality of rights. The Army's record in offering educational opportunies to men in the form of literacy schemes and rehabilitation programmes is well known and has a important effect on the development and functioning of soldiers. However, girl soldiers are rarely able to take up these opportunies (opportunities which change the social and economic expectancy of the soldier long after he leaves the Army). Selection procedures are more intense so that girls falling below a certain level of literacy are excluded. This does not apply in the case of male conscripts who expect to be given opportunities of improvement and who in fact see the Army as offering them opportunities previously missed. For men the Army is a total experience; for women it is *dilettante*, frivolous, trifling. This is not to say it is entered into in that way, but, on recruitment, when women realise the role they are expected to play, these are the characteristics which emerge. Exemptions are easy, deferment simple, release for one reason or another, uncomplicated. The women of the Army, far from being an integral part of the Armed Forces, are lent out to various Ministries, notably those of Absorption and Education to work in the integration of immigrants and in teaching in areas where teachers are in short supply.[5] The second-class nature of their role is clear. In their book on the Israeli Army, Luttwak and Horowitz refer in only two paragraphs and a footnote of one sentence to women in the Armed Forces. This is in a book of 446 pages.[6]

After the war the peace negotiations dragged on. At home the country began to assess the losses; hold a port-mortem on the battles; live and relive the horrors of those three weeks which constituted the October 1973 war.

In the obsessions with the aftermath of the war, the negotiations to find a peace, the recriminations, there was no inclination on anybody's part to express feelings about the pain the women left at home had felt. The country was busy making heroes, haggling over rights and wrongs, developing its hierarchy of war widows, bury its dead.

When the fighting was finally over, some women, including those in the Women's Movement, found themselves something useful to do. Always concerned with serving they offered to help at rehabilitation centres for soldiers, making coffee, serving food, playing *sheshbesh* and generally talking to the soldiers in an effort to help them recover from their traumatic experiences. Civilians were sent to the Fronts to provide various forms of relaxation for the troops, such things as lectures and seminars, which were intended to help towards readjustment. Women were again excluded from this valuable task, so that many women from the Universities and other professions with much of value to offer had no outlets for their experience and no chance of making a positive **contribution.**

11. The 1973 Election – Israel Reassesses

As life returned to a new kind of normality in a country greatly saddened and embittered by its experiences, the election campaign became a major issue once more. Postponed from its first date in October 1973, it was now due to be held at the end of December of that year. Parties had to start campaigning again. This campaign was to be a different one, however. Emotionally battered by the war, the people blamed their leaders and their generals for their unpreparedness. Arian writes: 'The outbreak of the Yom Kippur war on 6 October 1973 rudely ended the heady days of belief in Israeli invincibility which began after the Six Days War in 1967.'[1] All the feelings of disappointment, misery and frustration rushed to the surface and were heaped on the old guard, led by Golda Meir. The people wanted change, new ideas, vision and if possible, alternative ways of looking at their national predicament. After years of being too frightened for boat rocking, the establishment had itself violently, nearly capsized that boat. The mood of the people was despairing. They felt betrayed.

When electioneering resumed, it did so in the face of new issues and the emergence of differing values. Because of the huge losses in the War, the Army was ill prepared and slovenly, living too strongly on past glories. Because of the wastage of human potential, the paralysis of its women and lack of planning, the country's economy was at a near standstill. Arian writes:

> On the home front, acrimonious debate concerning the responsibility for the many shortcomings in preparing for and in handling the war attracted the public's attention ... Morale was very low, protest groups sprang up calling for basic changes in the handling of the country's affairs; there were strong calls for the resignation of the leaders in charge at the time of the war, especially Defense Minister Dayan.[2]

Before the war it looked as though domestic issues would dominate the campaign at last, offering a chance for newly emerging groups, including women, to have some say in their own affairs. Questions of internal organization and social reform had been in the minds of the electorate. After the War, though, the mood changed dramatically, the emphasis being on recrimination over the events immediately past, Israel's unpreparedness, the ability and integrity of the leadership and, above all, fear. The Labour Alignment, its back to the wall, fought on the only front it knew, that of security and the occupied territories. All the main parties had army officers on their lists of candidates, the right-wing alignment getting its share of respectability by recruiting Arick Sharon[3] and Ezer Weitzmann.[4] Because of the large number of officer-politicians, the pressing personal, domestic and social needs of the people, which had, hitherto, been of major importance, did not become a conspicuous part of the campaign. The almost total control of the political scene by the military inevitably excluded women from active participation as candidates. They were not wooed by the parties as nominees. Only the Civil Rights Party tried to fight the election on issues close to the hearts of the people and brought a feminist on to its list. It may be significant that the Civil Rights Party was finally able to put three members into the Knesset, including the feminist candidate, and Shulamith Aloni was eventually made Minister without Portfolio in the Rabin Government.

As was predicted the Labour Alignment remained the dominant party, but it had to face a government in which the Right of Centre Group plus the national religious group commanded a larger majority than the labour alignment. As a result, Rabin, when he became Prime Minister after Golda Meir's resignation in May 1974, found it to be in his best interests to collude with them whenever possible. This was further to erode the feminist voice. In the Knesset only Marcia Freedman[5] maintained a consistent position of raising the consciousness of Members on the needs of women. Although the Movement was growing steadily, its members had little political awareness and the Movement itself lacked political initiative. It was not ready to see feminism in terms of political activity. Many of Marcia Freedman's efforts on behalf of women were blocked by the Government as collusion took place between Rabin and the religious parties.

For the entire period of Rabin's Government[6] the country was absorbed by its problems of security and the enormous responsibilities and conflicts of the occupied territories. The War of 1973 heralded in the famous 'shuttle diplomacy' of Henry Kissinger, which bombarded the people's consciousness until the election of President Carter at the end of 1976.

Although immigration continued, Israeli nationals left the country in their hundreds, causing any attempts to maintain stability, establish traditions and encourage standards to be laid down virtually impossible. Because of the narrow, inflexible, blind position taken by successive governments, especially after 1967, and the country's financial dependence on the United States, there had been little economic planning. Jobs were becoming scarce, the philosophy had stagnated. The country was rendered powerless to create an autonomous, viable sovereign state in the Middle East.

In all spheres of public life corruption and malpractice emerged. Although, after the war, women began to express their feelings about what had happened to them, little was being done to remedy the situation or to bring women into the society as fully adult citizens. In one area though a breakdown came. The Egged Bus Company, the national bus cooperative, instituted a training scheme for women so that women drivers would be available in an emergency. Previously this move had been vigorously resisted.

Hostility towards the Arabs was kept simmering by trigger-happy military politicians with little understanding of politics, diplomacy or statesmanship. Gradually the Government became more and more out of touch with the needs of the people and made less and less effort to apply policies relevant to progress. As the security situation and Israel's credibility in international spheres worsened, the Government bombastically displayed their own fears and insecurities. The inability of the Israeli Jews to resolve their psychological battles with the Arabs had rendered them impotent to understand their own motivations and had not helped them to retrieve the situation.

With the emigration of Israel's skilled and professional class the electorate was slowly changing. The Old Guard Labour Party who had traditionally relied on the blind loyalty of the Ashkenazi sect was slowly being undermined by the new immigrants Sephardim, whose social, educational and human needs had been neglected since the formation of the State.

Constant exposures of corruption in the Government and among businessmen combined with the hopelessness of Kissinger's persistent forays into the Middle East worsened the situation. After 1975 the country began tentatively to reassess itself, but during that reassessment the Prime Minister's own weaknesses came to light, causing him to resign as a result of the exposure of his wife's financial malpractice.

A general election was called in 1977. Although women had organized themselves into a party to fight the election and had fielded a candidate, they were unsuccessful. The country decided to elect a right-wing reactionary government. Menachem Begin, the leader of Likud, became Prime Minister. The cult of manhood remained as Moshe Dayan, a life-long supporter of the Labour Party, was brought into the Government as Foreign Minister. This is the background against which we have to examine the beginnings of a women's movement in Israel.

PART TWO

12. The Start of the Women's Movement

The events of 1977 suggest that male chauvinism had reached its dominating position, but during the 1970s contrasting events within the country were bringing slower yet more lasting changes.

While Israel remained male-orientated, in Britain, France, the rest of Western Europe and the United States, women, after years of dormancy, were taking steps towards liberation. By 1971, when Israeli women at last began to form a movement, there was already a considerable literature of feminist books and pamphlets in English. Even among the uninitiated the names of Germaine Greer, Kate Millet, Jessie Bernard, were household words. Consequently, when Marcia Freedman and Marilyn Safer, two teachers at Haifa University, started the first seminars on women's issues in 1970 they had traditions on which to draw and already formulated ideas to disseminate and digest. These first seminars were dynamic. Well organized and run, they were attended by both Jewish and Arab women at the University and quickly demonstrated the need for more examination and understanding of the subject.

Early in 1972 Marcia Freedman informed the Press that a Women's Movement was being formed[1] and found herself inundated with requests for information. In Haifa alone, a group of supporters quickly formed to act as a nucleus for the embryonic movement and Marcia herself was invited to address groups of women throughout the country. Initially, the Haifa group concentrated their efforts in the area of consciousness-raising,[2] an important early step in the development of the movement in the United States. Consciousness-raising groups mushroomed in the town as women began to explore the possibilities of self-awareness, re-discovery and self-determination.

The first aim of the feminists was to try to built up a self-confidence which could be used for social change. To help this come about another event was taking place in Haifa at the same time. A group of women at the University started a campaign to open a day-care centre for small children on the campus. Day-care facilities in the country at that time were haphazard and scarce.[3] Although kindergartens were universally available, these were intended to provide only pre-school experience. Because of their hours of opening, the length of holidays, etc., they did not enable mothers to pursue any occupation or to study outside the home. Various women's organizations had, over the years, established day-care centres but these were over-subscribed and were mainly intended to be for women working in factories and for large over-crowded families.

For women who wanted to study and make a new career for themselves, and for women in all kinds of occupations apart from the most menial, there were few facilities. Many who worked made private arrangements, usually employing domestic helps.[4] For prospective students this was more difficult. University education in the country is expensive and the cost of this, coupled with payment for the care of young children, made the decision to study a difficult, even an impossible, one. None of the universities recognized the special needs of their female population, neither staff, employees nor students, and there was no viable provision for young children on the campus. The plan of the campaign was to obtain a room at the University plus a grant for the provision of equipment and the employment of a worker. The projected centre was to take the children from the age of one year on a sessional basis, fitting in with the needs of the mothers but providing a stimulating environment for the children. From the very beginning the project was opposed by the administration but victory was eventually achieved when the committee found itself supported by the newly elected left-wing student executive.

In March 1972, after protracted negotiations, a room was found, a small grant was provided, and the first University day-care centre in the country came into existence.

The day-care project and the start of the Women's Movement were not entirely synonymous, since the provision of day-care facilities are not necessarily a pre-requisite of a women's movement. However, it was not coincidental that some of the women in the women's groups were also involved in the negotiations over the day-care centre. Both Marilyn Safer and Marcia Freedman gave their support and time to the project. Marilyn Safer needed the centre for her own young child, although Marcia Freedman's daughter was already of school age. The inter-relationship between the day-care centre and the Women's Movement was, however, evident, since the women's ability to express their own needs in relation to their careers was encouraged and developed by the growth of female consciousness. From many points of view the issue was a fundamental one, for it brought into sharp focus one of the important areas of inhibition to the progress of women. Without day-care facilities women with young children are prevented from taking part in social activity at every level. The project was an exercise in which the women flexed their muscles for future activity. It helped them, too, to discover areas where they could expect support and those where hostility was obvious. It also gave them the opportunity of testing out that hostility, looking at its nature, learning ways of dealing with it.

While the battle over the day-care centre was raging, the more theoretical groups of feminists used the experience to analyse and assess the behaviour and motivations of their opponents and to distinguish the areas of opposition. The women were unfamiliar with political activity of any kind and this theoretical exercise, running concurrently with the practical exercise, gave depth and skill to the operation. It also tested and teased out responses to male–female antagonisms.

13. Consciousness-raising

From the very beginning, consciousness-raising became a vital and serious function of the Women's Movement. In the early days, while the day-care centre was still in embryo, the idea of using this technique in the development of the Movement turned into positive action. Several of the American Women's Movements had been using the skill successfully for many years but its relevance to Israel had been questioned. It was clear to the feminists that consciousness-raising groups in America had given women a badly needed sense of self and helped to develop the concept of sisterhood. Feminists in Israel were not fully committed to the idea of simply taking the American model and were searching for more direct reasons for using the technique.

It was not long before reasons were found. When the small group of feminists first came to express their ideas in public, they were amazed at the amount of hostility they experienced. And they were amazed at themselves for being surprised, for they were in a society that, no matter which ethnic group one looked at, had very positive, rigid, totally male-oriented ideas about the role of women.[1] And these views, from the lack of secular marriage to the emphasis on the birth of sons, right through the whole gamut of male chauvinism, were totally supported and reinforced throughout the country.

The feminists, then, committed as they were to what they knew to be a right and just cause, were tentative and nervous and felt themselves seriously threatened by the hostility they constantly encountered. As their views became better known throughout the small country, they were often taken aback by the change in attitudes towards them of neighbours, friends and acquaintances. The views of women had never been openly expressed in any of the ethnic groups, nor was there any tradition of listening to what women had to say. That feminists should want to express their views, views which were already becoming acceptable to other societies, and should want to have them understood and respected, required far greater consideration than this primitive society knew how to give. The women began to feel themselves cast out. They were often ridiculed socially and publicly or were given less serious consideration than would be given to a young child. The society did not feel itself committed to respecting its women as equals.

As Haifa is a town of around 180,000 people, the ideas which the feminists were expressing were slowly receiving some publicity. Their views were becoming as familiar as they themselves were. As the new Movement's aims became known, and the town realized it was the centre of this activity, panic set in. The re-interpretations of the arguments of the feminists were often garbled and uninformed. The women felt highly vulnerable. Those among them who were newcomers to the country felt particularly isolated. In a society with only faintly disguised initiation rights – those rights taking the form of participation in one or other of Israel's wars – these immigrant women felt uncertainty creeping into their feelings. They had come from the United States and England where their involvement in radical movements had been their lifestyle and where they had not experienced similar forms of alienation and hostility. Their new ideas, which in the outside world would have seemed positively conservative, in Israel were looked on as nothing short of blasphemous. The Zionist ethos has always thought of itself as advanced, one of the myths being that its men and women were equal. Now it was suddenly being faced with contradictions.

These women, conscious of their handicap as women, wanted to be understood. They wanted to have their views weighed and considered. They wanted to be treated as adults in an adult society. They could not accept the narrow, paternalistic, traditional view of life which the country held so dear. They knew this traditional view was not good for women of the country and they wanted at least to have an opportunity of expressing themselves. But if they were given this opportunity the society would find that those who, for generations, had only been allowed to remain little girls would very quickly grow into women. Israeli men, both Jews and Arabs, have had no experience of women. They recognise only mothers and little girls. When Golda Meir was described as the 'best man in the Government',[2] the joke misfired. This was in fact the only way this narrow society could describe a woman of power, maturity, reason, resourcefulness, decisiveness, etc. These were not qualities they had ever been prepared to see in the females they knew, even if such qualities existed. In Golda Meir they were forced to recognize them.

The women of the Movement, then, were faced with a form-idable task. They were feeling totally alienated by the culture, a culture into which many of them had been born, and which they were at the same time pressing to change. To women outside the Movement the ideas they were expressing sounded interesting, but to act on them carried too much responsibility and demanded much disruption. To be an adult woman in Israel, where no such concept existed, was almost inconceivable. Maturity carried with it all kinds of responsibilities, disciplines, standards. In more ad-vanced societies room is made for women to grow towards this. In Israel, if it came it would come quickly, bringing enormous prob-lems. Many women were frightened. In their own homes, too, the feminists did not always find support and tranquillity. For some marital relationships became strained, and close family loyalties were on trial. Outsiders were suspicious, arguing that the women of the Movement were lesbians, could not get men (although five out of the seven women in the caucus group at that time were married and living with their husbands) or were interested only in promiscuity. Socially (and the country's lifestyle is very de-pendent on social relationships), life became very difficult for them.[3]

They lived mainly among the middle class of the city. This was their peer group. But it was a social group with little flexibility or ethnic mobility. It was one in which married couples entertained married couples either at parties or at small fairly formal coffee evenings where wives vied with each other over the best cakes; the men talking to the men and the women to the women. Many of the feminists had their roots in the town. They had gone to school there, grown up with the same contemporaries and were fully aware of the expectations that family and society had for them. Others, the new immigrants, needed acceptance from newly formed friends and acquaintances, wanting to integrate, wanting in the first instance to feel part of this society and to be liked and accepted. The country and the city expected a lot from their immigrants, a great deal of money was spent on them by the State and they were expected to conform.[4]

When they were invited to private social events the feminists found the conversation always turned to the subject of the Women's Movement even though they themselves never instigated this kind of discussion. Then the men would become hostile and abusive, fearing their wives would be 'corrupted'. Often the other women in the room were frightened of their own feelings when they heard what the feminists had to say. While the feminists were expressing radical views for which they often found a spark of sympathy from their fellow women, they refused to maintain the highly circumscribed life-styles of these women. Israeli women prepare and serve food obsessively and continuously – if not for children, husbands and relatives, then for friends at self-inflicted social gatherings. At social evenings in their own homes they provide several different kinds of cake – all home made – tea, coffee. Many take pride in being able to say that they have never bought a cake from a shop. Throughout the whole society this ritual is repeated week by week, year by year, for the whole of their lives. It is the *raison d'etre* of the whole female society. At social evenings they compete with each other over the lightness of their sponges or the creaminess of their chocolate *gateaux*. In this way they attain some form of recognition, some form of achievement, some form of creativity, in a society which holds none of these attributes, manifested in any other form, as priorities for women.

The feminists refused to compete in this way. If they attended these social evenings they talked with the men, failed deliberately to ask the hostess for her recipes and would not get involved in the discussions of the latest births, marriages or deaths. If they entertained reciprocally, their husbands often served the guests and made the coffee. The food, if any was provided, was bought from a shop. The feminists were determined to demonstrate alternative

ways of behaviour for women which would give them freedom
and room for manoeuvre. They dressed differently, behaved
differently and spoke of different things. One even smoked
cigars.

These may seem trivial matters which could not change the
course of history, but they have to be seen in the context of Israel
– a small conformist society. The formal kind of lifestyle described
above is common to most of the Jewish women in the country.[5]
There may be less formality among the less well-off with relatives
rather than friends being entertained, but the principles remain
the same. Indeed, a lot more food is served. A lot more work is
done in preparation. The 'serving' subculture binds them all. But
whereas the Jewish women entertain heterosexually, having some
involvement with the group they are serving, the Arab and Druse
women entertain only male groups, serving but taking no part in
the entertainment. The Druse women are not allowed even to
enter the room when guests are present.

The lives of the vast majority of Israeli women were rendered
useless except in the kitchen and in bed, so that it was in these
fields and in the allied one, related to both, of serving, that Israeli
women obtained most of their satisfaction. This is the area in which
conditioning has played its greatest part. No matter how diverse
the personality of the women, how deep their aspirations, how
strong their individual needs, what their likes and dislikes, how
radical their thoughts, how intense their feelings, the women of
Israel were unaccepted, rejected and emotionally destroyed, if they
did not conform superficially to the good housewife and mother
image. Jewish and Arab societies have always subjected their
women to a one-dimensional life. No regard is paid to the prefer-
ences of women, to their skills, their creativity, their ideas. If they
achieve some status in the world, their families are not proud of
them and they receive little acclaim. Jewish and Arab women have
been schooled for centuries not to disrupt the society created by
men for men. They have moved forward, undoubtedly, but only as
the men have allowed. They are ignored in every way it is possible
to ignore them. The men of Israel did not feel that they need to
adjust or bend to any of the deeply felt emotional needs of their
wives and the women had no way of making the men do so. They

had been too well conditioned, too cowed, and had become too resigned, too weak to fight for alternatives.

Until the feminists began to experience all these pressures and to realize how they themselves were being affected by them, they had not thought the lifestyle of the people would affect the dynamics of the Women's Movement. They had not expected to bring about a conversion in the nature of the society overnight, but they were clearly unprepared for the hostility they experienced and the violent feelings they encountered. Unprepared, that is, because they seemed to be receiving two different messages. On the one hand their views, behaviour and ideology were seized upon by many women in the town, but on the other hand these same women could not bring themselves fully to absorb the new ideas and greeted them with highly ambivalent feelings and behaviour. It was as though the spark started by the Movement must be fanned very slowly and obliquely lest it cause fire which was uncontrollable.

The feminists had few weapons with which to fight their battle. They wanted to form a Movement which would grow and become important, but they were quite unprepared for the amorphous battlefield. There were few allies outside the small nucleus. Women in general were frightened by their own responses to the views of the feminists. The feminists, too, had been conditioned by the same pressures and traditions as their erstwhile sisters. They were confused by the responses they were experiencing. They had little ammunition to use against this society which, when they had conformed, had loved them, but which now abused them, refused to listen to them and gave them no respect.

The Israeli feminists of the 1970s had not experimented with other radical movements as had their American and British sisters. There had been no 'civil rights' movement as there had been in America in the 1960s. Political developments had been formal, conformist and male oriented. The feminists, therefore, were not only putting forward new ideas but were demonstrating new courses of action to which Israeli society had not yet become accustomed. In this conflict, consciousness-raising groups were play a vital part.

The groups continued to flourish, new ones being formed

continuously. Some reached certain crisis points as members dropped in and out. Most groups were not static throughout their existence and this caused a variety of problems. First, a consequence of this fluidity was that groups were unable to move on past an initial stage of self-discovery. Most groups when they formed would spend several sessions with each member discussing her personal history (or those parts of it which she felt strong enough to express). She was able to take as much time as she liked over this. All the other members were free to question, intervene and discuss various points as they arose during the monologue. This served to offer people a common ground on which to meet, since most women expressed feelings and described events which they had never had the opportunity of doing before. For most women, guilt and shame at their own intense feelings on a variety of events and incidents suppress their ability to communicate such matters. The next stage then is to work on some of the areas which seem to have a common theme and to develop self-knowledge and work through this process. To know that one's responses to incidents and experiences are shared offers comfort and strength. However, when a group did not remain cohesive over a period or whenever new members began to participate at any point, the group had to return to the first stage of its deliberations. It also took time to learn to trust a new member and to draw that new member into the group and to absorb her. When a member left, a similar process of disturbance took place – the group having to come to terms with this loss and the resultant feelings of anger, disappointment and mistrust at the lack of commitment of the absent member.

All the facts were present all the time in the formation of the early groups. Joining a consciousness-raising group in Haifa at that time was fashionable, trendy, the 'in' thing. Women felt that identification with a group was the automatic password to liberation – it was all that was needed to turn one into an emancipated woman. In fact, this was far from the reality. To gain from a consciousness-raising group demanded stamina, commitment, strength of purpose and dedication. Much of the exploration undertaken in the groups raised painful feelings and disturbing responses, uncovering hidden shame, guilt and uncharitable feelings. These were important revelations of self, but they needed acceptance, trust, love and sisterhood to be used valuably. These bonds took time to form and only those who remained constant to the group for several months were able to benefit fully from the experience.

The structure, then, of developing groups which were more closed, more circumscribed in terms of membership from the beginning, began to emerge. Among the old stagers a feeling developed that women indicating a wish to join a group should be matched with each other before starting. This idea, however, was never adopted. Although it was mooted, no time was put aside for working out criteria for assessment nor for organizing a register or list of applicants. It was probably also felt that initial enthusiasm would be lost if bureaucracy took over in a field where natural spontaneity and extemporization were essential.

In general male political movements do not face these types of problems. They hold their interest by the political theories they express. Political theorists do not have to face the kinds of question which attack their own individual identity or which make them uncertain of their role and their sexuality. Indeed the reverse is often true, for male political theorists and successful (or unsuccessful) revolutionaries often have their roles and their sexuality reinforced by their actions and beliefs. Violent movements contain within them, for a time at least, a romantic image which is self-perpetuating and feeds the egos of the people who support and control them. Political achievement is in itself highly satisfying to the individual as it greatly enhances the sense of self, releases the individual from mundane chores and elevates him to a position of superiority. As races and religions carry their own brand of machismo so do political movements. And the machismo is essential to maintain motivation of supporters and to enhance leaders. Why is it that leaders of movements are usually dressed in uniform and have hazy female figures in the background of their lives, not always made explicit, but inferring a normality and romance in sexual relationships? Male political movements thrive on these images and appear not to be able to function without them. In fact, political movements based on the importance of a male leader have a host of traditions and standards on which to draw. They basically follow each other in their behaviour patterns and tread the well-tried path which thrives on man's need for a paternal figurehead, offering authority, responsibility, identification and power.

Women's Movements have no such tradition. There are few leadership models to follow and with which to identify. There is little in the way of accepted practice. In the past Women's Movements have had little success and have not sustained themselves for very long. Generally women have joined together to fight a specific injustice – the vote, contraception, etc., – rather than in support of liberation. Since most campaigns were fairly short-lived, personal motivations were not unduly dominant so that there was little time to play power games. As soon as these games took precedence over the cause itself, the Movement tended to disintegrate. Women have not been conditioned to devote themselves to the development of the ego. They have always been told that their main fulfilment comes with marriage and childbirth. So they are expected to submerge their needs for political success, power, dominance. At worst women marry revolutionaries, visionaries, fanatics – they do not become them. Natural excesses of this kind appear obscene if they are characterized in women. It may be for these reasons that feminists have always looked to men to support them in their cause and have allied themselves to more universal radical movements. These radical movements seemed sympathetic, but in general the women's problems never became important in the movements they supported. The cause of women's liberation has never been recognized as a cause worthy of major political considerations and actions – except by women. It does not carry the status and charisma of world revolution and Marxist–Leninist theory. It may be that revolutionaries do not identify directly with the causes with which they are fighting; they are fighting for others and this has an air of selflessness about it. The women's cause is universal to women, embracing even those who are its main exponents. It is not a question of the articulate middle class fighting for the under-priviledged proletariat. It is a question of oppressed women fighting for themselves.

For women to join men's political movements is dangerous to

the feminist cause. The women can never succeed in achieving their aims as their aims will always be in conflict with the aims of the men and those areas of life which will revolutionize the lives of women can never be areas which will fire the imagination of men. Martyrdom for men is personal sacrifice opposite the barrel of a gun. For women it is life lived under severe physical and emotional stress with no outlet and understanding, as well as constant discrimination. The man's condition is easy to identify with and to romanticize – the woman's is too painful to contemplate and carries a stark reality.

Women then are not fighting for someone else. Their cause does not exist on fantasies, half understandings of other people's lives which need changing. They are fighting a cause directly concerned with themselves. If they win their battle, then they themselves would benefit along with everyone else.

14. The Spread of Feminism to Jerusalem and Tel Aviv

As consciousness-raising groups settled into a permanent feature of the Movement it became clear that some of the groups were not satisfied simply with the activity of introspection and started to look for projects to focus on. One such was an analysis of Israeli children's books to study role structure and identification. This was modelled on a similar project which had usefully been undertaken in the United States. Although started in 1972 by a small group of women in Haifa, the project became the subject of a degree dissertation of one of the group members.[1] Several years later it was used by the women of the Tel Aviv group in discussions with the Ministry of Education on the subject of sex stereotyping in children's books. This project helped the women to take steps to look at the wider society and to begin their first tentative approaches towards greater political activity. At that time, too, the idea of a library of books on the subject of women was born.

Although the women were beginning to organize themselves they still had very little money, no premises, and no central address. As a result the library was established with donated books and a set of second-hand bookshelves. Within a short time there were dozens of books on the shelves and a well-maintained catalogue. The library soon became an important facility, not only to women of the Movement but to researchers, students and others wanting more information on general and specific aspects of women's liberation and consciousness. As well as the project concerned with sex bias in children's books, and the library, other groups were involved in information-gathering and fact-finding as the idea for a newsletter was conceived.

Gradually the Movement took on a more political, activist character, and developed a two-pronged focus. On one hand, consciousness-raising groups spawned, spread and flourished with interested women in other towns forming similar groups and using similar techniques, as women travelled between cities to share views and discuss experiences. At the same time other (sometimes the same) women began a political prong concentrating on activist proposals, policy making and organizational methods. The original nucleus groups remained paramount in this activity, retaining their original form for weekly consciousness-raising sessions, but moving outwards and drawing in other interested women to develop the political aspects of the Movement. No opportunity was lost for discussions of principles, aims and ideas, drawing in new members, explaining the ideas, politicizing, getting support, making their views known. At the beginning of the summer of 1972 a committee had been created in which two members of each consciousness-raising group were invited to participate. This committee met regularly once a month, holding semi-public meetings to try to form some semblance of a national movement. From this committee, Marcia Freedman emerged as the leading figure, with the result that the Movement began to have a shape, a name and an address as a focus.

From the early days of the day-care project and throughout 1972 the women continued with the gathering and dissemination of information. They were continuously asked to speak to other groups of women. The non-religious political parties began to show an interest. As a result of some publicity in an American newspaper a wealthy American benefactor offered money to Haifa University to be used by the women for specific projects. Unfortunately the mismanagement of this offer by the University authorities, who took the negotiations out of the hands of the feminists, created hostility and antagonism and the offer was withdrawn.

Yet, in spite of this setback, the feminist movement was growing, its radical ideas seeping through to the hitherto closed society. As a result, on a personal level the women, both the activists in the Movement and those who were involved only through the consciousness-raising groups, began to experience problems. Their involvement in the Women's Movement had given them a personal commitment which came into conflict with their traditional role in the family and in society. To question current ethics and values, especially when those ethics and values have been around for several thousand years, evoked hostility and aggression in husbands, lovers, families and friends. For some, an open indication of their commitment to the Movement alienated them. While the women were showing their willingness to open up to radical ideas, the men of that society took much longer to reach that stage. This created difficulties within families and between couples. For single women the transition was even more painful. The role of the single woman in Jewish society is a difficult one, since the only expectation for a single woman is to marry and produce children. Because of the considerable and overpowering pressures put on them to conform, most are unable to withstand this coercion and succumb, often making unsatisfactory marriages and living unhappily ever after. Those who, in spite of everything, remain, for one reason or another, unmarried, do so in the face of serious rejection, loss of ego-strength and personal guilt. They were not second-class but third-class citizens, reaping few rewards from a society which sees them as ugly failures, crippled in some way and deserving of little consideration, respect or human understanding. Subtly they were insulted, cast out, denigrated. A woman without a husband is without identity.

When the Women's Movement became a reality in Israel it provided a place of safety for many single women. It allowed them to be themselves, to pursue their own needs, feelings and strengths. It accepted them unconditionally and, above all, offered a loyalty and understanding which they had previously not experienced. The Women's Movement and the solidarity of its ethos allowed for emotional growth in the women.

In the same year, 1972, and throughout the early months of 1973, the Movement spread to Tel Aviv and Jerusalem. From the start these two new branches took on their own individual characters. In Tel Aviv many of the women who showed initial interest were already involved with politics, mostly with the Civil Rights Movement. Their more sophisticated political expertise led them naturally to develop their abilities to organize politically, to be aware of political advantages and to use opportunities as they were presented. Their businesslike, organized approach tinged with the valuable shrewdness fundamental to political activity allowed the Tel Aviv women to see the power possibilities in feminism. While the Haifa women were still developing a feminist consciousness, the Tel Aviv women were perfecting their already considerable organizational abilities. They did not use consciousness-raising as their jumping off point and it was some time before they saw it as an important aspect of the growth and development of feminism.

The Jerusalem Movement emerged almost in the same way as the Haifa group, some of its women also having returned from trips abroad where they had come into contact, for the first time, with feminist concepts. They developed yet another strand. In what was traditionally the seat of learning and the centre of academic achievement, the women of the Jerusalem Movement reflected this trend in their commitment. Fact finding, philosophizing and the academician's wary approach to new ideas were the attributes they brought. Gradually these three quite different groups began to amalgamate, offering each other expertise in their own particular field. By early 1973 a public debate on women's issues had started. In January the newspaper *Davar* published excerpts from a discussion held by a group of Mapai activists on the subject of women in Israel. The discussion defined some of the primary areas of institutionalized discrimination and raised issues of wage and salary differentials, lack of training for women and the problems of trying to combine home and job, resulting in many women having to work part-time and thus harming their career development. It was becoming clear that women outside the feminist movement, while not expressing views which were entirely new or revolutionary, were, for the first time in many years, addressing themselves to the problems of women in Israeli society. These women advocated the need for change, feeling that women should be encouraged and expected to participate more in the political and social institutions of the country.

Gradually, the ideas which had slowly been developing and which had started from a mere handful of women in Haifa a year or so before, had become those of a Movement. The library in Haifa was growing, both in its collection and in the demands which were being made upon it. Regular general meetings were being held and the women of Haifa and Tel Aviv were working together to produce a small news sheet which appeared towards the end of 1973. The main task of the newsletter was to assimilate material on feminism, give information and discuss feminist ideas. There were also book reviews and other criticisms.

From one of the first news sheets the following offers some insight into the picture of women in Israel in 1973:

1. The average female worker in light industry (food, textiles, ceramics) receives 30 per cent less than the male worker for the same work. This is based on definitions of the same work in different ways as standard work and light work. The women always do light work and are therefore paid in accordance with separate pay schedules. 2. In Germany and America, 50 per cent of women of working age work outside the home. In Israel, 30.2 per cent work; this is only 3 per cent more than in Egypt. 3. In spite of the fact that there exists a law of equal pay for men and women, enacted in 1964, the average monthly earnings of a male wage earner is 750 I£, of a female 500 I£ (1972 figures). 4. Workers compensation for men and women cost the same in terms of monthly deductions from their pay, yet women receive payments that are 10 per cent less than men. 5. 50 per cent of the members of the Histadrut are women. There are only three women among the 40 members of the central committee. 47 per cent of the Labour Party are women. Only two women in the Knesset are representatives of the Labour Party. In all parties, only 8 per cent of the Knesset members are women.

As the Movement grew and more women allied themselves to the cause of female emancipation, feelings began to run high. In Haifa, where the Movement started and was, probably, due to Marcia Freedman and the other pioneers, at its most vociferous, feminists were becoming recognized on the streets, in shops and in cafés. By the summer of 1973 groups of feminists were to be seen sitting in street cafés, in the open air, in clusters, with supporters, fellow travellers, uncommitted interested followers. Their controversial ideas and lifestyle became an irritant to the conventional, conformist society in whose midst most of them lived. Insults were heaped on them by men, husbands of wives sympathetic to the Movement but too nervous, too timid, to commit themselves, and by men aware enough themselves to know that the very existence of this Movement was a threat to their peace of mind and their security.

For, predominantly, women's liberation is about feelings. To take the initiative, to gain independence, to achieve individuality, mean understanding of oneself and of others. Conformity is concerned with smothering feelings, with decrying spirituality, sensuality, emotion, involvement. Nationalism, too, demands set stereotypes and uniformity. Feminism is the antithesis of all this. It is concerned with the exploration of self, with growth of personality, with shedding these imposed stereotypes, with examining accepted lifestyles, with questioning male precepts, male superiority, with discussing and exploring sexuality, motherhood, domination, sexual repression, psychological oppression, inadequacies, the whole realm of female experience which the Israeli woman carried on her back with vast responsibility in the early 1970s. All these things, plus politicizing and fact-finding, were the preoccupations of Israel's Women's Movement by the spring of 1973.

Yet, in spite of this activity and signs of consolidation the Movement still lacked authority. The Army remained bumptious, assured. Its general air of casualness and its aura of controlled negligence had become institutionalized. The image appealed to Golda Meir, offering her the chance to play the grandmotherly role.

The men had not changed. Only the women, those in the Movement, and those who gained strength just because the Movement existed, had changed. Their institutions were being broken down and no disasters were occurring because of it. The timid were becoming dominant; the oppressed were slowly beginning gently to become liberated; the isolated were becoming embraced; the weak were beginning to feel stronger. From the beginning, press and television had been interested, somewhat tolerant and in some measure supportive. They were, at least, prepared to listen to the women and report their activities.

In 1973, too, the first ideas for the Women's Centre took shape. Women's centres had been a concomitant of most of the Women's Movements in other parts of the world, offering a physical centre for women to meet, exchange views, gain information and develop. In Israel, also, the idea of a Women's Centre had been part of the original plan but little had been done about it. However, by 1973, the women were ready to consider the possibility.

At the same time the national election campaign began. Elections for the Knesset were due to be held in October of that year. This was an important opportunity for the women to exercise their newly found political skills. At a local level the Municipality of Haifa showed an interest in the Women's Movement, not because it felt there was any need for immediate involvement but because with a little vision they felt it had a part to play in the future of the country. The *Ma'arach*, the Labour Alliance, had, by tradition, always had one woman on the City Council. That woman was resigning and Marcia Freedman, now the most well-known and politically conscious member of the Movement, was suggested. However, the suggestion was never followed through. The ideas of the Women's Movement did, however, filter through to Moked the Democratic Communist Party and it used its influence to ensure a representative on the Women Workers Council.

As the general election campaign slowly got under way, the Women's Movement became more consolidated and made plans for even greater involvement. They attended any meeting where candidates were appearing and raised the issues of the feminists. Politically, they saw themselves allied as a body to Shulamith Aloni's Civil Rights Movement Party[3] as that party appeared to be the most closely identified with women's rights through Aloni's work on civil marriage and other issues. However, in order to remain politically independent, no obligation was put on individuals to vote for the Civil Rights Movement Party or to feel committed to it. The policy was generally only that the Civil Rights Movement Party seemed to be the Party which was most likely to be sympathetic to the aim of the Women's Movement and therefore it should be given a chance.

The Tel Aviv group, however, did see itself as a section of the Civil Rights Movement Party, insisting on attending every meeting of the party, following its policies and ensuring that it became well known and an influential splinter group.[4]

As the lists of candidates were assembled, Marcia Freedman was invited to become a member of the Civil Rights Party list. The Women's Movement was able to produce the number of signatures required to ensure her nomination and she was being strongly wooed by the Party. But even at that early time the motives of the Civil Rights Movement Party were becoming quite clear. Shulamith Aloni in spite of her record on behalf of citizens' rights had never actually shown any solidarity with the women's cause and this became even more obvious as the campaign began. Before the lists were drawn up, activists of the Civil Rights Movement and the Women's Movement worked together to assemble the list in time for the nominations. When, however, the list was established, the representatives of the Women's Movement found themselves patronized and victims of condescension. At the first meeting of the election campaign, many women attended to give support and to raise the question of the platform on women's issues. The leadership of the Party (Shulamith Aloni was not present) was very happy to see so many women there but immediately tried to deflect them from their serious political purpose. It was suggested that the women make the coffee and they were offered feminine roles unconnected with the issues. There was a great deal of flirting by the men and such remarks as, 'How come you don't smile?' were bandied about.

From the beginning of the campaign Marcia's position was ambiguous, since she was concerned only with feminist issues and not with the wider issues of the Civil Rights Movement. Presenting Shulamith's committee with the feminist manifesto after her nomination, Shulamith assured her that the Women's programme was not only unacceptable to the Party but to the country and the electorate as well. 'It would alienate women,' she said. She accused Marcia Freedman of not knowing how to conduct herself in politics. From her anger it was clear that she felt out of control and that she was battling with a force – feminism – which she had underestimated. In its efforts to gain the women's vote the Civil Rights Movement had not thought through the implications of Marcia Freedman's nomination. They had assumed, in some ways correctly, as it was to turn out, that by simply having Marcia Freedman on the list, the Civil Rights

Movement's involvement with feminists would, by implication, be
clear. They were not prepared to confront the electorate head-on
with new, radical thinking about women. For her part, Marcia's
agreement to stand had been based on other suppositions. She had
wanted a more positive commitment by the Civil Rights Movement Party to the women's issues. She wanted to demonstrate that
this was the only party committed to the overthrow of oppression
of women in the country. She also wanted to ensure that these
new concepts were not lost and to have the opportunity of airing
them in the campaign. From the standpoint of the Women's
Movement her nomination to the Civil Rights Movement list had
been seen as very important, offering a whole new area of political
activity for women and a national voice through which they
could speak and be heard. She had wanted to put together a
women's vote which would enable them to go out on the streets,
pamphleting and campaigning purely on women's issues. This
volte-face on the part of Aloni meant for Marcia Freedman and the
Women's Movement a re-appraisal of their position not to support
the Civil Rights Movement Party at the coming election. Some of
the Haifa women continued to be active in the campaign and
gained political experience and expertise – much needed at that
time; others remained loyal to previous political affiliations.

The Tel Aviv women, already in general committed to the Civil
Rights Movement Party, continued to be active in the campaign.
However, they, like Aloni, were not committed to Marcia Freedman's point of view and had little contact with her during that
time. By September 1973, when the campaign began and the battle
between Marcia Freedman and the Civil Rights Movement Party
started, the political superiority of the Tel Aviv women became
obvious. What was not very clear then was the strength of their
commitment to feminist principles and to Civil Rights principles
nor was it clear where they put their priorities. In some ways this
lack of clarity, the situation in which the edges of the two philosophies were blurred, in that the Movement was unsure where the
Tel Aviv women stood, sowed the seed for much of the trouble
which was to come later and which delayed the cohesion of the
Women's Movement.

The Yom Kippur War had affected the feminists too. In groups throughout the country they began to share their experiences of the war weeks. They had much in common. All felt neglected, left out, ignored. But worse than this, maybe, their fight for self-determination and the self-confidence which they had begun to develop before October 1973 had been seriously undermined.

As the election campaign continued the humiliations of the war were being verbalized. Throughout the country women were talking about what had happened to them. Through this dialogue other aspects began to emerge. Useless as the women had felt themselves to be they, nevertheless, realized the strengths which they had been able to use at home. As they had taken over completely at a domestic level, they found they did not need to turn as often to their husbands for the small tasks which needed doing at home. The men, too, returned from the fighting, were becoming conscious of their own changes.

For the women of the Movement and for Marcia, the fighting of the earlier campaign was far from forgotten. Shulamith Aloni and the Civil Rights Movement Party were still anxious to have the backing of the Women's Movement, since it could make a difference to the number of votes cast, but they wanted it on their own terms. Also, the general mood of the country had changed. Now, there was a mood for change, for new ways of thinking (not yet, maybe, for revolution) and the Civil Rights Movement found itself with more popularity than it had expected.

As the campaign progressed, it became clear that the Civil Rights Movement Party was going to have little to do with presenting the viewpoint of the women or with publicizing any of the demands of the Women's Movement. However, the outcome expressed clearly the mood of the people. Marcia Freedman's name

on the list of candidates attracted the votes of women and many,
even those with little or no contact with the Movement, voted for
the Civil Rights Movement Party. Their percentage of the poll
gave them the right to have three representatives in the Knesset.
The third on the list was Marcia Freedman and her election was
confirmed.

Marcia's election to the Knesset brought changes in the
Women's Movement. Because of her lack of knowledge of parliamentary procedure, her difficulties in expressing herself in
Hebrew, a newly learned second language for her, and her complete inexperience of political life, combined with the traditional
life-long erosion of her confidence, which had relentlessly pursued
her, Marcia felt unable to do justice to any other forms of political
activity and resigned the Chair of the Women's Movement in
Haifa.

With Marcia removed from the centre of the scene the Movement was left in a difficult position. Leaderless, the Haifa women
felt more vulnerable than ever. Marcia's election had been an important event for them and had given them status in the town and
in political circles generally, but it had left them leaderless and
they had difficulty in once again assuming a role. The Tel Aviv
women who had, in the main, been instrumental in ensuring
Marcia's election were very anxious to ensure that she toed the
line.

By the time the war came, the Jerusalem women were having
little influence on feminism and even less on the Women's Movement. Marcia's election helped to re-activate them. Her seat in
Parliament meant that she needed to spend three days of each
week in Jerusalem. She shared a flat with one of the original Haifa
members, Shoshan Ealings,[1] and was able to continue her feminist politicizing there. Almost immediately, two consciousness-
raising groups started. These brought in other people, many of
whom were already on the brink of feminist thought. In 1974 the
Jerusalem Women's Movement was ready to start again after its
early, faulty steps in 1971.

The early months of 1974, as the feminists jolted themselves out
of their dejection, were important ones for the women of the
Movement. In Haifa, Tel Aviv and Jerusalem, activities specific to

the character of each group took shape. In Haifa the chair was taken by Malka Maon, who was an active feminist and an ardent supporter of the Movement, but her career as a psychologist and changes in her personal life caused her to find the task impossible after a short time. In many ways this was a useful situation as the Movement then decided to move towards collective leadership and an effort to bring about a different form of organization was tried. In the beginning the Movement seriously missed Marcia's leadership and drive. But when she finally gave up her position of prominence the Haifa women were forced to look for alternative methods of carrying on the impetus of the Movement.

One important project, the last that Marcia was involved in was the Women's Centre. It united the women of Haifa. Although this had been tentatively suggested several times before the hiatus of October 1973, it was not until March 1974 that it became a reality. Two events influenced it. First Malka Percal, one of the original group and a student at Haifa University, had been to Europe on a visit the previous year. During her time in Amsterdam, she had visited the Women's House. She was impressed by its organization, its ability to attact women and perhaps most important of all, the behaviour of the women whom she met there. 'Suddenly I got the feeling of what it was like to be where there are no men,' she said, 'the difference in the way women behave made me see them differently from the way I had seen them before.' On her return she decided that the setting up of a Women's Centre was to be her commitment to feminism. The war of 1973 intervened but in the following March things were sufficiently back to normal for her to return to this commitment. In the meantime Marcia Freedman had been in the United States where she had been given a few hundred dollars to help with the Women's Centre.

Malka Percal and a few other feminists found a suitable building. In order to put the new idea of a Women's Centre across, they decided to hold a series of eight lectures on topics of interest to women. The programme was worked out, posters contributed by a feminist artist were designed, printed and distributed and the project was started in June 1974. The opening event was a short feminist theatre piece, followed by a talk on it by Marcia. Using masks and mime the actors portrayed the experience of being a housewife. The performance attracted between sixty and seventy people.

As expected, the tableau created interest and engendered criticism. 'It drew the image of the housewife as a mixture of a device for producing babies, a maid, whore, idiot, a passive woman whose only desire is to please the bread-winning male master.' One critic, Dalia Avnion, in an article entitled, 'Who is the truly liberated woman?'[2] expressed some of the latent hostility. It had certainly raised questions. The hallowed role of housewife and mother was under scrutiny. She adds:

... one can conclude that a woman shaping pots is happy and contented while a woman who chooses to shape her children's character is miserable and frustrated. They (the women of the Movement) ignore the fact that the biological characteristics of human beings are not equal and neither are their needs. Maybe, if a woman relinquishes the possibility of giving birth she will become free to race along with men on her professional career with no obstacles. She had better sterilize herself and so avoid bringing into the world another unwanted creature, for, if it is a girl, she will become miserable, frustrated and oppressed by men, and if a boy, he will grow up to be evil, possessive and exploit women ... I myself agree with Bernard Shaw who said, 'Equality between men and women will not come until women agree to give up their rights.'[3]

For the first few months the Centre thrived. All the planned lectures were well attended. The library was rehoused there. People could obtain feminist literature and newspapers. All help was provided voluntarily. Women set up a rota to service the Centre in the evenings so that there would always be women there at specific times to answer questions, to offer legal advice and to provide a limited form of citizen's advice to women. Very quickly, though, things began to go wrong.

As a meeting place and advice-giving service, the Centre quickly failed. Situated far from the centres of women in need, it remained inaccessible and remote. In such a home-based family-orientated community there was no tradition of women meeting each other outside the home in the evenings or at week-ends on a regular and frequent basis. Socially, people visited in couples, single women either staying at home or searching for men friends or similar status enhancing activities. The idea of an information service seemed like a good one but inquiries did not come and the women who took turns to sit in the Centre on two evenings each week quickly became discouraged. As long as the posters were distributed, women came to the meetings, many women joining during that time. However, money for publicity soon ran out and with it ran out the flow of women to the meeting-place. They struggled on for about a year until finally in the summer of 1975 the Centre closed.

But in Tel Aviv, at the same time, other activities which helped to consolidate the Movement there were being developed. Immediately after the General Election in 1974, the Tel Aviv women had to spend some time in coming to terms with the new Civil Rights Movement member in the Knesset – Marcia Freedman. From their point of view there was some confusion over her role in relation to themselves. At first, since they had worked hard to ensure her name on the list and were instrumental in helping towards her election, they felt she was obligated to defer to them in all matters. Marcia saw her role as being autonomous once she was elected and some time had to be spent by both sides to establish this principle.

Marcia clearly defined her loyalties as being divided between her concept of feminism, as she had worked it out over the years, and her commitment to the Civil Rights Movement Party of which she was now an active member. Until her involvement with feminism in Israel, Marcia had been free of any political commitment and had not seriously considered herself in relation to any political colour. Her election made her face her responsibilities. But she needed time to define clearly her strategy and her allegiances. This difficulty and her newness to the role of politician added to the strain of her already difficult relationship with the Tel Aviv women. They began to mistrust her and to suspect her motives, although at that time she was taking stock rather than influencing events. Even though she made her position clear to the women in Tel Aviv, they were unsympathetic.

At the same time as this battle was going on the other feminist groups were taking much strength from Marcia's role. With her in the Knesset, they began to concern themselves with matters of national significance and of fundamental importance to women. in January a proposal for a new law concerned with civil and human rights and, more particularly, equality for women, came before the Knesset. This engendered considerable discussion, interest and debate throughout the feminist groups and in the newspapers.

In May Marcia Freedman and Rachel Alterman, a leading radical feminist, wrote an article in the newspaper *Ha'aretz* discussing the new proposals. They referred back to the Female Labour Law, 1954, and accused it, along with other discretionary laws of that time, of over-protecting women. 'It implies that a woman is a weak creature who needls "protection". The law in this case is a guardian rather than an "enabling" device.' They went on to say that:

the existing law concerning confinement leave is another example of over-protecting women. This *prohibits* anyone from employing, for money, a woman during the period of twelve weeks after giving birth. A woman who is not entitled to National Insurance money does not even have the right to go to work. Arguments of health are not valid here as floor washing at home is not any easier a job than teaching or writing a thesis.[4]

They contended that the law of 1954 was based on an image of woman as a feeble creature not mature enough to be responsible for herself.

In another article in *Ma'ariv* Marcia referred to women as a social group in distress. She looked at the position of women in the country at that time and considered the various areas of employment, job prospects, education, Army training, to be examples of serious discrimination. All this, she felt, indicated that the distress of women had a political basis.

The elementary human rights of a democratic society – the right to life and freedom and for seeking happiness – are too often denied to women. The only way of self-definition for her is pairing with a man so that, in exchange for her services, his way will be hers and his achievements, hers. For most women marriage is the only means of guaranteeing themselves social and economic security and a way to social mobility in the grown-up world.[5]

On what she described as 'the housewife's symptoms', she referred to research showing that clinical depression is twice as frequent in women as in men. The 'housewife's illness' is seen as depression, constant fatigue, a tendency to accidents, lack of interests. The illness has no social stratification and is classless. Its causes are many; boredom, uncreative and unrewarding work of a routine nature, social isolation, lack of challenge and expectation, lack of status or prestige, dependency and no self-evaluation and self-development. These are exactly the signs of characterizing a socially and economically distressed group. Seventy per cent of women in Israel are defined as 'housewives'. She added:

Naturally, there are exceptions. But the social problem is not defined by and therefore not solved by relating to the exceptions. Putting the blame on those who are not among the exceptions is a way of disregarding the oppression of women and is misleading. We have to find out the real cause of women's distress and abolish it. However, there is something to be learned from the exceptions. Most of them are single women. This fact clarifies that breaking ties with the ruling class (men) can be one of the prerequisites for rescue. The status of women is not a private problem of one woman but a political and social problem that is being neglected in Israel, since we still refuse to recognise its existence.

In this statement, made a few months after her election, Marcia Freeman made public her philosophy – her commitment. She had brought women into the political and public arena.

16. Abortion

For the Movement, the early days of 1974, and the election were difficult times. Rather than making their task easier, the election of the first feminist (albeit under the banner of the Civil Rights Movement Party and not women's emancipation) made the Movement throughout the country uncertain, its future course equivocal. In Haifa the change in the leadership was a set back. In Tel Aviv there was a need to change expectations and to rethink their relationship with Marcia. Only in Jerusalem, after a series of false starts, was the nucleus of a movement taking shape. Clearly a unifying medium was needed and that presented itself when the Abortion Campaign got under way.

At that time, the position on abortion was anomalous. Illegal though it was, it was readily available in the private medical market for anyone who could afford to pay for it. Like many other areas of life in Israel, the knowledge that abortions were extensively carried out remained an open secret and the authorities had traditionally turned a blind eye. According to the middle class who benefited most, the system worked well and there was little need for change. Again, they had always had the money and the know-how to operate this semi-underground system which for them was a straightforward 'abortion on demand' policy. However, the secrecy and clandestine nature of the subject kept the matter hidden, thereby taking out of the public arena an important and serious issue which was of great national significance. The acceptance of a system of illegal operations of any kind denies the possibility of control, either of cost or of health factors. It totally suppresses public constraints and limitations and inhibits government and medical management of the subject.

As a result abortion fell into the realm of peasant medicine. There were no records kept of how many abortions were per-

formed each year; the number of poorly executed abortions resulting in death or serious, permanent injury to the mother; the
ease or otherwise with which the under-privileged and poorer
sections of society obtained abortions; the cost and whether the
standard varied depending on what was charged; the standard of
post-operative care. The field was one which operated totally outside the realm of public scrutiny and was an area beyond that of
general social justice and impartiality.[1] It was essential, therefore,
to bring it into the mainstream of Israeli life, to legalize it, and
as it was an important and necessary function of the society, to
enclose it within the general provisions for medical-welfare.

The feminists had tried to mount a campaign on the subject
during the previous year, before the war. However, it had gained
little impetus, so the signatures they had collected and the literature they had produced had been put away for another effort at a
later stage. That time came in the summer of 1974.

A committee which had been sitting for two years discussing
the issue of abortion was about to publish its recommendations
and these were to be put before the Knesset in the form of a Bill.
Politically this was a good time to develop interest in the subject
and bring about changes. The make-up of the Government meant
it would be possible to force a freedom of conscience vote. In this
way, without Party discipline operating, there was a good chance
of a majority of Knesset members voting for some kind of abortion
reform.

The feminists wished to publicize these recommendations, to
encourage public debate, to consider a counter-Bill which Marcia
wanted to put forward in the Knesset and to get as many signatures as possible for legalizing abortion. Clearly, from their
point of view any Bill sponsored by the Government would be
more conservative than they would wish and they were not prepared to let an unacceptable Bill go through by default. The
women stood on street corners obtaining signatures for their petition. They lobbied Members of Knesset, gaining attention for
their views. The petition campaign brought in some 30,000 signatures. All the time Marcia worked with them. Through her
contacts in the Knesset; by being there day by day; knowing the
correct timing; talking to Knesset members; lobbying; being

around with antennae extended; getting to know political correspondents; 'softening up' journalists by giving them information
about women's issues and the Women's Movement, she was able
to lay the foundation for a sympathetic hearing when the abortion issue was floated.

The women of the Movement developed the philosophy for the
Abortion Campaign. They spread the notion that adults had a
right to decide the fate of their own bodies. The slogan 'My body
belongs to me' eventually became an important part of the campaign. Several demonstrations were held, attended by small groups
of women but given large coverage by television, the medium
which, up till then, had been consistently sympathetic to the
Abortion Campaign. On one occasion a demonstration of about
ten women was given coverage out of proportion to its size. Once
the television reporters and cameras waited over an hour for a
parade of women who were expected and who had been delayed.
The feminists felt they had established a public consciousness on
what was seen as an expressed demand by women.

Finally, the two Bills came forward for preliminary vote in the
Knesset. One, drawn up by Marcia, was to permit abortion at the
request of the woman within the first three months of pregnancy
with no conditions whatsoever stated. After that, termination
could only take place under three conditions:

1. Danger to the life of the woman.
2. The possibility of a deformed or severely handicapped child.
3. Pregnancy as a result of rape or incest.

The second Bill was drawn up from the findings of the
committee and recommended abortion on approval. It listed many
conditions under which abortion could be approved and included:

Unmarried women under the age of seventeen and over forty-five.
Life and death of the mother.
Difficult financial or social situation.
Deformed foetus or the birth of a severely handicapped child.
Psychological considerations.
Pregnancy out of wedlock. (This created an enormous loophole for
   married women, who could go before the committee stating that the
   expected child was not her husband's. This was termed 'out of wed-
   lock'.)

At first it was recommended that a committee of doctors should approve the abortion but that proved controversial to the committee and the decision of who should approve was left out of the first draft.

Both Bills passed the preliminary reading and were then referred back to the committee for re-drafting.

Without the large campaign mounted by the Women's Movement Marcia's Bill would have been killed. First reactions to it were violent. Knesset members considered it 'scandalous'. They could not understand the concept of women making this decision for themselves. They talked of permissiveness. They objected to women demanding control over their own bodies. For the women the important issue, repeated over and over again, was a human being's right to control what happens to her body and what her future will be. The other issue, often expressed, was to make clear what is involved with pregnancy, birth control and abortion.

But the women were not only talking about abortion. They were bringing into the open all sorts of taboo subjects – pregnancy, birth control – subjects, which, after all, were about sex. The main clash both within the Knesset and outside it was with the religious parties, although in the early days these had failed to react as violently as prophesied. In the beginning they appeared not to take the whole campaign very seriously, ignoring as usual the expressed demands of the women. When they finally saw the seriousness of the feminists' fight it was too late for them to effect much control over the situation. On the Government's Bill they insisted on a few changes in more liberal areas, but in general they had 'missed the boat'. Clearly the women of the Movement had identified an area with which many of the women of the country were in sympathy. With many of the more abstract, cerebral theories of the Women's Movement the majority of the indigenous female population found difficulty in empathizing. This issue, however, was immediate, dynamic, practical and highly topical, affecting them very immediately. Marcia gained great strength from this, knowing that she was unequivocally speaking for a large proportion of the women of the country – only women with political power were against abortion on demand.

17. Prostitution

The abortion campaign had lasted about four months. Hard on its heels Marcia found herself faced with the issue of prostitution. A Bill was introduced by the Government making a woman liable to one year's imprisonment for constituting a public nuisance when she is out on the street for the purposes of prostitution or for being a traffic hazard when she is out on the pavement for the purposes of prostitution.

The Bill was slipped quietly on to the Agenda. However, having noticed it Marcia speedily and vociferously whipped up support among colleagues to oppose the Bill. By the time the session started the Minister of Justice knew that it would cause considerable discussion in the House and that many would speak against it, even people in his own Party. The subject was taken off the Agenda and a meeting was called of those members interested in the subject. There were about seven or eight members present, including Marcia. The attitude which prevailed was that something needed to be done about the problem of prostitutes on the streets but that the Bill was a punitive one rather than one which would help to create social reform of some kind.

Until that time little discussion of prostitution had taken place within the Women's Movement. However, Marcia and some of the feminists had discussed the issue. For them prostitution epitomized and encapsulated the whole phenomenon of oppression of women.

From the point of view of the prostitutes there were vital issues which nobody was at all interested in. The facts were that the majority of prostitutes were young girls, some very young. About 25 per cent were between the ages of fourteen and eighteen, and 57 per cent between eighteen and twenty-five. Almost all came from the Asian and African communities. Many had been school drop-outs and had run away from home at an early age, because the home environment had been intolerable. In general they came from the most severely socially and emotionally deprived areas of society. They had drifted into the life without having received any understanding and support and were ripe for any form of exploitation.

Marcia had met some of the prostitutes and was concerned for their well-being. Many wanted to give up prostitution, but had no means of livelihood nor anywhere to go. They lived in constant fear of the pimp, and the police – sometimes, even, of the client. However, their self-hatred and self-destruction rendered them impotent to bring about changes in their life-style.

With a small group of Knesset members Marcia raised the question of 'institutionalizing' prostitution. This could take the form of zoning laws, re-establishing and legalizing brothels, health supervision, rehabilitation services of a real kind, to help women who wanted to get out of the work, and ways of helping them to free themselves from pimps, using the police as a protective service for the prostitute rather than as a harassing agent. Much of this Marcia was able to get across to this group of Knesset members. Finally, a compromise was reached. The Minister of Justice agreed to bring back the Bill for it was clear something needed to be done about the nuisance created by prostitution on the streets. It was also agreed to appoint a committee to study prostitution in depth and to focus on the area of women in distress.

When the Bill again came before the Knesset, Marcia spoke against it and she and a few others voted against it. She had put forward an amendment calling men – the clients – to account, but that amendment was lost. The Bill, in its earlier form, passed the preliminary vote, but was referred back to the committee to await the outcome of the commission.[1] For Marcia and the feminists the issue of prostitution raised many questions regarding men's sexual standards and morality. She intended to put some of these questions to the commission.

Since the views Marcia put forward were feminist arguments, she thought the Women's Movement would be in agreement. However, the Tel Aviv women were very angry at the stand she had taken. They did not want prostitution legalized and were in favour of abolishing it altogether. Marcia, too, felt that not to have prostitution was by far the best solution. Yet this could not be done by legislation, only by offering women alternative opportunities and expectations. If better possibilities, education, lifestyles, were available to them, they would then have no need to prostitute themselves. This approach may, on the surface, appear to offer simple solutions to a phenomenon about which there is still little understanding. However, this inability of most women to develop by their own efforts a lifestyle of the type and at a level they would like, makes prostitution not a last resort but a means of escape into a form of freedom. For those who are able to accept this way of life, prostitution offers independence and self-determination of a unique kind. That it contains within it its own dangers and limitations is a fact, and it is in this area that the first steps towards reform need to be taken. For the rest, reform is still at the talking stage.

1974 was ending. The year had seen the growth of the Women's Movement, its first Knesset Member, the developing expertise of consciousness-raising. Central issues such as abortion, prostitution, birth-control, were entering the national consciousness. Earlier, the first consciousness-raising group had started a project to look at sexism in children's books. Useful work was done. However, at that stage it gained little publicity and contributed nothing to creating a change of attitude. At the end of 1974 Marcia started to raise the issue again, coupling it with a question of sex discrimination in schools. This had been a preoccupation of hers for some time, for in May that year,[2] in an article in *Ma'ariv*, she had pointed out the discrepancies which were taking place in the field of higher education.

Among graduates, thirty-seven per cent are women; among postgraduates, twenty-four per cent, and among Ph.Ds, sixteen per cent only. Women as a social class are 'sub-employed'. That is, they are employed in positions well below their standards of intelligence, professional training levels, work experience, education and seniority. No methodical research had been undertaken but the position was clear to see. Women with Ph.Ds teach in high schools and secretaries with twenty-five years' experience do not achieve management positions.

International Women's Year was officially inaugurated in Israel by the President, Ephraim Katzir. In a ceremony held at the President's residence he, Prime Minister Rabin, and the Speaker of the Knesset, Yisrael Yeshayahu, signed a scroll proclaiming 1975 as International Women's Year. The Declaration read:

> Declaration of International Women's Year
> For the Promotion of Equality Between Men and Women

In fulfilment of one of its true and profoundly humane functions the General Assembly of the United Nations, in a resolution adopted on 18 December 1972, has proclaimed 1975 as International Women's Year, during which period Member States are asked to endeavor to promote equality between men and women, to ensure the full integration of women in the total development effort and to recognize the importance of women's increasing contribution to the development of international friendship and peace.

In full agreement with the objectives of this Resolution, we hereby initiate the observance in Israel of the year 1975, 5735 in Israel's calendar, as International Women's Year.

Let us in 1975 strive to eliminate remaining inequalities, to facilitate the dual role of women in the home and at work; to acknowledge the joint responsibility of parents; to facilitate women's attainment of their full potential and encourage them to enter political and public life in greater numbers.

We call on Israel's women themselves, heirs to their great historic traditions, to utilize more fully the opportunities available to them, and on men to aid and assist them in their commitment to public and economic life.

We call on Israel's institutions, governmental, public and voluntary, to cooperate in making International Women's Year in Israel constructive and meaningful through practical programs of action, through legislation, through the application of existing laws in both the letter and the spirit, through education and through the provision of incentives and services for women, to enable them to play an ever greater part in the development of our country and in the advancement of a state of peace in which children of this area and everywhere may grow up without fear of war.

EPHRAIM KATZIR   YISRAEL YESHAYAHU   YITZHAK RABIN
President   Speaker, Israel   Prime Minister
[Parliament]

But in spite of these grandiose intentions, International Women's Year did not much affect the work of the Women's Movement, neither helping nor hindering it. Remaining mainly, as in most other countries, a public relations operation, the feminists were not called on to participate in the Year nor were they invited to attend the prestigious Mexico Conference. The Conference was attended by Mrs Rabin and others. International Women's Year ran concurrently, rather than in association with, the work of the feminists.

1975 was, for the feminists, the year of challenge. In that year they brought their fight out on to the streets. It was the year of demonstration and confrontation. These were the women who, four years earlier, had been so frightened that they met in secret and discussed in private issues which, in 1974, were raised by their one brave Member of Knesset. In 1975 they, themselves, the feminists of Israel, in their own right shouted these issues in the streets and aired their views in the market-place.

The issue which incensed them in the first months of that year was in an area of life which they had not previously examined in detail. This was the religious influence and the important part it played in helping to maintain the female stereotype.

For many years, even among men, it had been felt that the Jewish religion was the most important factor in repressing progress of all kinds. For the so-called liberals, and those who had broken their ties with their religion and their religious forebears, the Rabbis had become a scapegoat and could be blamed for any kind of inquities in the society. Clearly, the religious leaders of the country, and the political parties which they supported, had a large influence on the life of the society – an influence probably far greater than the numbers of people who believed. And it was clear, too, that the Labour Party, the majority party in the Knesset, was and always had been very concerned to placate the religious parties (a minority in the Knesset) as often as possible since every vote in the coalition government was vital. It was the religious parties who, early in the life of the Knesset, at the time of the Ben Gurion premiership, together with the Arab representatives, ensured that women would be excluded from combat in times of war and it is on religious grounds that women (and in extreme cases, some men) can obtain exemption from Army service.

In every-day life the country defers to the religious leaders and their influence is strongly felt and greatly respected. Rabbis sit in the Knesset, religious festivals are the national holidays; there is only one day of rest, Saturday, the Sabbath, and the nation accepts religious observance as a sacrosanct part of its existence.

The religious parties run their own schools, their own crèches, their own adult education centres and their own organizations to encourage and spread religious ideas. Among these ideas is the belief in the importance of large families and the non-acceptance of abortion and birth-control. The Welfare Ministry, too, is controlled by the religious parties, ensuring that an illiberal approach is maintained in matters relating to social services, for wherever initiative and change interferes with religious principles and observances, that change and initiative is blocked. Not for nothing was the Western Wall the pinnacle of achievement in the liberation of Jerusalem in the June War of 1967.[1] By the same token, that Wall, a national monument, not a synagogue, has become a shrine of the religious fanatics, being divided off as a large area for men and a small area for women. What other national monument would be allowed to maintain this discrimination?

The Knesset itself can take much of the blame for this for it is the Government which passes the laws, not the religious leaders. One such law which is particularly iniquitous to women is the law in relation to marriage and divorce.

All laws relating to relationships between husband and wife are religious laws and are administered in accordance with *Halacha*. They are, however, passed by the Government. There is no civil marriage or divorce in Israel which among other things makes inter-marriage between couples of different races or religions virtually impossible. Only proven Jews can marry according to Jewish law, Moslems, or those prepared to be Moslems, according to Moslem law, etc.

Yet iniquitous as this may be, in general the people have always remained ambivalent about the influences of religion. The deep traditions and knowledge of some kind of religious teaching through parents and grandparents for most Jews in Israel, together with the knowledge of centuries of religious persecution, has had an effect which cannot be underestimated. Even for enlightened Jews, the narrow, oppressive influences of their forebears have been hard to shake off. The very country itself, manifesting evidence of the religious tradition through six thousand years, from Haifa and beyond in the north to Masada in the south, symbolizes a faith which defeats the humanists, rationalists and non-believers. Yet its power is recognized. Elon writes:

> The power of the theocrats has been enhanced in recent years by the revival among secular politicians, socialists and liberals, of a curious, quasi-religious piety. A kind of sentimental religiosity has seized the former rebels against orthodox religion and talmudic observance. They do not necessarily return to the orthodox fold. On the contrary, they often remain flagrantly non-observant; most Israeli politicians never, or rarely, go to synagogue, nor do they keep a kosher home. They will often eat pork, violate the Sabbath, and give their children a secular education. Their newly found religiosity is an atavistic, sentimental, almost mystic character. It probably reflects the deep psychological crisis of an ageing power élite, and in some cases borders on chauvinism and racism. The combination of orthodox piety among the secular political élite and the direct political power of the clericalist parties has dominated the Israeli legislature in recent years and has caused the erosion of principles formerly held by the secular majority.[2]

Of all the Jewish religious laws created to oppress women, the laws of Halacha are the worst. Implicit in them is the fact that the woman is the man's property. Therefore, only the husband has the right of granting a divorce.

Since divorce is obtained through the Court of Rabbis, they have the power to grant or withhold a divorce as they see fit, according to the evidence and the religious law. As a woman is legally her husband's property, upon his death, if there is no male heir, she becomes the property of his oldest living brother. She may not marry her brother-in-law, but if she wishes to remarry she must obtain his release and he can refuse to grant it until he receives a considerable share of the widow's property, including pension and compensation which she may receive by law as a widow. If the brother-in-law is a minor, she has to wait until he comes of age. If he is in a country to which she has no entry, she then has no power to remarry.

In the Rabbinical Court women are not allowed to testify. Only men have that prerogative. In one case, for instance, there was the question of dividing the property between husband and wife. They had been in business together, both taking an active part in building up the enterprise. In the divorce proceedings, the husband testified that the business was worth a certain amount of money. The woman, to outsiders, said it was, in fact, worth four times that amount but she was not allowed to testify and did not receive a fair share of the proceeds. Often the man will try to incriminate his wife by hiring a private detective and a photographer to catch her in the house with a man. The wife is unable to testify or bring other people to testify that she is not, in fact, having relationships with other men. A man can actually live with another woman and have a child by her, yet his status as far as the divorce is concerned is not affected. Conversely, however, a woman cannot even have a conversation alone with a man in her home, when the couple are separated. Should she do so she is considered a 'rebellious wife' and may lose all her rights to property, children, alimony, etc. If she leaves her home during divorce proceedings, she also loses her rights. Her husband does not, and even if she is being constantly ill-treated she has no redress. In addition cases can drag on for several years, since it is in the interests of husbands to delay the granting of a divorce and thereby delay the paying of alimony. Delaying tactics frequently used are; that he will try to be a better husband; that he wants a reconciliation, etc. This is usually granted and he returns to the Court at regular intervals reiterating these requests. During this period he is often not even living at home or is using the home to

suit his own purposes, leaving the wife dispossessed and tyr-
annized.

In cases where women are continually beaten by their husbands,
the Rabbinical Court does not usually consider this grounds for
granting a divorce, particularly if the husband apologizes and
agrees to turn over a new leaf, often having no intention of doing
so. Throughout the divorce proceedings a woman must agree to
sexual intercourse with her husband, since she is expected at all
times to fulfil all the duties of an obedient wife. If not, she is
'rebellious'.

It was this series of laws which the feminists found intolerable
and on this issue they intended to hold their first demonstration –
in Haifa, outside the Rabbinical Court. At the same time, other
factors were causing society to question the religious monopoly
over marriage. Shulamit Aloni was still pressing for a Bill to bring
in Civil Marriage. The week before the demonstration the
Supreme Court overturned a practice of the Rabbinical Court.
This was that if a woman had a lover and her husband divorced
her because of the lover, this was stamped on her divorce
certificate and she was forbidden both to the ex-husband and to
the lover. She therefore could not marry the lover if she wanted to.
This overruling by the Supreme Court was given press publicity,
so drawing more attention to the injustice and discrimination of
the Rabbinical Court.

At the same time the scandal of the 'black lists' was published.
These were lists of names of people who, for all sorts of reasons,
were debarred by the Rabbis from marrying. The list was compiled
on the basis of rumour, gossip and hearsay yet its repercussions
were very serious. Should someone have a grudge against a person,
it was only necessary to make up stories about them – for instance, that she was not Jewish – let the Rabbinical Court know,
and she was black-listed. Little checking was undertaken, but
when the accused came to marry she would find herself unable to
do so. These lists were circulated by the Rabbinical Court. There
was much protest in the newspapers.

All these incidents, spread over several months, reinforcing the
women's feelings, boosted their resolve and a demonstration was
held. It took place in June 1975 and was the opening shot in the

Women's own campaign of self-assertiveness as a Movement and in the continuing dialogue being held by many groups to press for a fairer system. Organized entirely in Haifa and attended only by women from the Haifa Movement the demonstration was hurriedly arranged. It was a noisy event, with the women with megaphones encouraging others to offer testimony in the street. The megaphone was passed round, too, to women onlookers, who wished to express their own feelings and affirm their identification with the demonstrators.

For the Haifa Movement it was very important. All the organization had been undertaken collectively by a group of women who had shared all the tasks and had divided the work. Whereas, previously, most activities had fallen to one or two women to complete, causing a large amount of work to be covered by a few people, this project had been divided up between many more, bringing about greater involvement. It had been dynamically conducted; the working group and the demonstration had been peopled by many women university students, with backgrounds of radical politics, developed abroad – mainly in Europe. A gathering of this kind outside the Rabbinical Court had not been seen before. As a result the religious leaders of the National Religious Party began to become aware of the existence of a Women's Movement, and to realize that there was a growing dissatisfaction with their monopoly over marriage. Unfortunately, this new understanding did not result in immediate liberalizing of views but in fact, and perhaps inevitably, caused a considerable swing towards a greater conservatism and reaction. However, alternatives were being considered and the whole scandalous business was being brought out into the open for the first time.

That the women had used this episode to test their ability to take more positive action on events and issues which affected them, was evident. Traditionally reticent and timid, they had always contained their resentments within themselves, never stealing the limelight or causing embarrassment to husbands and family. Overt activism in the form of street demonstrations and conflicts tears apart the hypocrisy and demonstrates to the whole world, in these days of instant media recognition, the grievances and discontents of the demonstrators. It also identifies, publicly, these women, wives of respectable men. Jewish women have, for a long time, protected their fathers and husbands from needing to look at and thereby take responsibility for, the oppression of their women. Demonstrating had been a hard step to take. It had needed an issue over which there was very deep feeling to activate the women. That issue had not concerned events of the moment but was directed at the root of their torment. The hold which religion had over the core of their lives was being tested. Since the beginning, observant Jewish men, each morning in their blessings have pronounced '*Baruch atah Adanai elchaynu melech ho-alam, she lo asanee ishah* – Praised be the Eternal our God, Ruling Spirit of the universe, who did not make me a woman.' This insult was beginning to take on a new meaning.

The six months leading up to that demonstration had been busy ones for the Movement generally. While the Abortion Campaign in the previous year had been progressing, the women of all three branches of the Movement were continuing with all their various, more long-standing commitments. Consciousness-raising remained an important, on-going task in Haifa, Tel Aviv and Jerusalem. Groups formed, failed, re-formed, providing a continuous dialogue on the subject of woman's role in society and keeping the subject alive in the press, on radio and television. In the Knesset Marcia pursued other issues which she saw as relevant and reported back to the Movement at every opportunity. Information-giving and spreading became a necessary function. The Movement's newspaper, called *Nilachem*, started in 1973, stopped during the War, and began again in 1974. This newspaper, produced mainly by the Tel Aviv and Jerusalem women, was widely distributed and helped to clarify the aims and ambitions of the Movement.

The Tel Aviv women, conscious of the need for feminist literature in Hebrew, decided to work towards publishing an anthology of the writings of women in other countries, mainly the United States and England. Entitled *Woman, Women, Womanliness (Isha Nashim, Neshiot)* it was edited by Rinah Sheleff, Sara Silkes, Shulamith Kaufman, Honey Meir-Levy and Margarit Weinberger. It was the first full publication of the Feminist Movement of Israel and appeared in 1975. Amongst the papers were articles by Shulamith Firestone, Jessie Bernard, Betty Friedan, Zoë Moss. Much of the time spent over the anthology was taken up with raising money to pay for its publication. The anthology itself was well received, sold out its first edition and was reprinted.

By the time 1975 arrived the Movement was becoming a force in the land. Three years previously it had been unknown. By 1975 it had established itself as a serious, deep-thinking group of women concerned with change in the country. Still small in numbers, it was beginning to feel itself to have some power and influence.

The Movement's impact on Israeli society was dramatic. Its growth had been swift and its development significant. For the first time issues rarely discussed before were being openly raised. Feminism, emancipation, liberation, were discussed openly by groups of both men and women in social gatherings, on radio and television and in the press. Gradually, in all the Universities, requests were being made for seminars on feminism, people were reading feminist literature, familiarizing themselves with the works of well-known feminist writers in the United States and England. But as well as this, and probably just as significant, the Women's Movement had opened up the possibility of discussing subjects in the whole area of life devoted to feelings. It was in this field that, until the Movement started, Israeli society was most unsophisticated and most polarized. The society thought of its people as strong or weak, brave or cowardly, responding as stereotypes to the various pressures which attacked them. Grief was institutionalized,[3] pain (in all its manifestations) was controlled, homosexuality, promiscuity, pre-marital sexual relationships were, according to official Israeli opinion, non-existent. The problems thrown up by adultery, divorce, alcoholism, prostitution, family breakdown, were, in the main, swept under the carpet.

After the war the men, too, were beginning to think about their own roles, about their reaction to the fighting, about themselves as individuals rather than as part of the Army machine. The new understanding of themselves which the feminists were expressing were forcing the men to think in different ways whether they liked it or not. Soon a dialogue started and continued throughout the country at many levels, at various stages of acrimony, both privately and in the wider context of the community. And this involvement activated discussion of other subjects. Subjects which on the face of it appeared to be peripheral were, in fact, equally important, for a society which oppresses women in the way that Israeli women were being oppressed, not violently, but by closing them off as human beings, would tend to treat other weak groups in similar fashion. So that liberation meant liberation for other groups also. Suddenly homosexuality, lesbianism, prostitution, sexual repression, obscure sexual practices, were being discussed seriously. The society which had denied the existence of homosexuality was developing a freer, more open attitude to the subject. Previously one of the country's great taboos, its existence was now being admitted.

Some women were beginning to think in terms of communes and the first of these was formed in Haifa in 1974. For the first time since the very early pioneering days a few women in the country began to choose to have children out of wedlock, to keep them and bring them up alone. This was a great break with tradition and opened another avenue leading to greater freedom of expression and a more spacious concept of self-determination.

In Haifa the Women's Coffee House was started; salvaged from the ideas behind the setting up of the Women's Centre it took the form of a community centre for women and was held regularly each week. At first Marcia's apartment was used and women met there for coffee and social contact. Used by committed feminists, it served a useful function in creating a regular, informal meeting place. The use of a private apartment for what was essentially a community provision had limitations so that numbers remained small and the centre did not quickly achieve popularity.

By 1975 the flair, enthusiasm and impetus within the Movement moved from Haifa to Tel Aviv and Jerusalem. The founders of the Movement in Haifa had, by then, split up. Of the seven original members, two had gone abroad. One, Marcia Freedman, was spending much of her time and energy in Jerusalem, using her sojourn in Haifa to concentrate on her private and domestic life, holding on, as far as was possible, to privacy and seclusion for herself and her daughter. She was living permanently apart from her husband by this time and was concentrating on creating an acceptable *modus vivendi* for herself. The rest, strengthened by their experiences, were individually striking out in society, pursuing ambitions, sowing wild oats long needing to be sown, establishing themselves in the community. The original consciousness-raising group did not reconvene after the October War, but some of its members continued to meet in an informal way. So desperate had been their need and so dynamic had been their group experience that they were all ready to find different forms of expression. By 1975, they no longer felt the need to cling to each other for support. Their fear had turned to courage and self-reliance.

19. Demonstrations and the 'Hilton Affair'

In the previous year Marcia Freedman had withdrawn from actively participating in the Women's Movement, apart from her involvement in the Abortion Campaign. By 1975, however, she felt sufficiently confident of her role in the Knesset and her position in the Party to return to some involvement. In the country hers was still the only authoritative voice on feminism to be picked up by the media and she wrote articles, gave interviews, spoke in high schools and at kibbutzim.

In Jerusalem consciousness-raising groups were mushrooming, ideas were being consolidated, the Movement was growing and the women, old and new members alike, were revising and familiarizing themselves with the areas of injustice which they needed to identify. Marcia, who had made her acquaintance with the Jerusalem feminists during her first year in the Knesset, was continuing her association with them, offering what support she could and developing healthy and useful links between her role as a Knesset member and as a feminist.

For her part, she remained a controversial figure in the Knesset but, by 1975, was beginning to gain credence, respect and support not only within the Party but outside it as well. She continued to raise and support important radical issues related to the needs of women and of feminism and maintained a feminist position.

Most active work in Israel usually takes place during the autumn, winter and spring, since the hot summer consumes energy and creates a national lethargy. But from January until June the Movement gained strength. On two kibbutzim, groups of feminists were emerging and were beginning to form feminist groups. The Tel Aviv group was busy working on the anthology. Consciousness-raising groups were continuing – new ones starting, old ones developing. New projects looking at various aspects of oppression of women were being initiated. New suggestions were being floated. One such, the storming of the Western Wall in Jerusalem to remove the barrier separating men and women, was explored and after much soul searching rejected. A group of women, some from the United States where they had been active in feminism, formed their own group to start a dialogue on their particular problems as women committed to the discipline of living their lives by a religious philosophy. Cautious steps were being taken all the time to try to unify the Movement and make it into one cohesive force. There were still many differences between the three centres and these were not easily reconciled.

Spurred on by the success they had had at the Rabbinical Court demonstration, the Haifa women met and agreed to try to mount a national demonstration to protest about the inactivity over the Abortion Bill, at that time still in committee. Two women went to Tel Aviv and Jerusalem to discuss the possibility.

In January Shulamith Aloni had put in a Civil Rights Bill. This was in effect similar to the American Civil Rights Amendment. Aloni's Bill took the operative sentence from the Israeli Declaration of Independence which prohibits discrimination and added to it the proviso that the Bill cancels out all laws which discriminate on the basis of sex, but excluding all legislation aimed at protecting pregnant women and young children. During the first few months of the year the Bill moved easily and smoothly through its various stages. The Labour Party had, after all, been involved with the wording of the Declaration of Independence. It could hardly oppose such a proposal as this, since it was itself committed to egalitarianism. The Tel Aviv women opposed the Bill on the grounds that the 'protective' part of the legislation was detrimental to the progress of women. They wanted to see more radical changes in the role of women in industry and were pressing for this.

When the Bill arrived in the Knesset in July for preliminary reading, it was passed without much trouble, only the religious parties, in the main, voting against it. For them, however, this was a serious setback. Within hours they announced that these were grounds for a coalition crisis. The next morning Mr Rabin, the Prime Minister, declared that the Government would not support the Bill. The news became front-page headlines. Rabin had clearly sold the women down the river for the sake of narrow political gains. It was obvious that the Bill was going to be buried in committee and had no chance of seeing the light of day.

Instead of concentrating on the abortion issue, the Tel Aviv women asked the other groups to support a national demonstration on the burying of the Civil Rights Bill.

Arranged for 21 October 1975, the women of the Tel Aviv Movement used the long, very hot summer to plan the action. They called on no one else for assistance and advice and organized it down to the last detail on their own. The format was to be that of a mock funeral for the Civil Rights Bill to be held in front of the Labour Party Headquarters. As part of their publicity campaign the organizers sent out notices in the form of funeral invitations. (In Israel it is customary to send out suitably sombre invitations to funerals.) During the whole period of planning and decision making, there was no consultation with either Haifa or Jerusalem.

Two hundred women participated, many coming from Haifa and Jerusalem. Only one small detail was ignored. The demonstration was unlicensed. Having applied and having had the application turned down, the organizers decided to proceed without sanction by the police. They also failed to mention this to the assembled demonstrators. The demonstration had little time to get under way when it was quickly attacked and broken up by the police. Undue violence was used by them, with women being manhandled and injured in the mêlée. This unprovoked attack threw them into disarray and caused anger and hostility. What was intended to have been a peaceful expression of feeling over a serious subject had ended in chaos and confusion. Four women were arrested. These women were accompanied to the police station by thirty other women who sat-in until their colleagues were released.

The newspapers reported the event extensively, with news coverage on every front page and sympathetic supporting articles. Journalists sympathetic to the Movement identified themselves for the first time, interviewing participants, providing background features on the event. Television did not report it at all and radio gave it only brief coverage. Reasons for this were never explored or explained, but a connection and sympathy between the Labour Party and the television and radio networks may have played a part.

The demonstration, in its unexpected show of militancy, had been very successful and had gained the sympathy of women and of uncommitted feminists. For some time afterwards there was euphoria among the women of the Movement throughout the country. The post-mortem on the event lasted many days. That the police had seen them as a threat was considered a victory for feminism. As well as feeling confident about future action, the women began thinking in ways they had not considered before. Confrontation politics clearly offered some form of authority and had a value far beyond the immediate action. The demonstration had united women and turned the Movement into a recognizable and acceptable force among them. Women who, previously had had nothing to do with the Movement and had not taken it seriously – university women, journalists, women in entertainment and the media – showed their solidarity. A second demonstration was planned. Based on the earlier Haifa initiative it was to be a combination of issues, particularly equal rights and abortion. They hoped there would be a wave of demonstrations. This time the Haifa women wanted to be involved in organizing it. Marcia agreed to help and offered to get the license and to use her connections where she could. It was to be held during the festival of lights, the feast of Chanukah celebrated each year around Christmas to commemorate the recapturing of Jerusalem by the Maccabees from Antiochus in 164 B.C. and symbolizing freedom for the Jews. This festival of lights was to be a torchlight procession and was to symbolize freedom for women. It was to be held in Tel Aviv.

About five hundred people attended. The women were singing, shouting slogans, carrying banners, holding torches. The Press was well represented. Delegations of women came from the two newly formed women's groups in the kibbutzim. About forty men marched with them. There was no violence. There was also no media coverage. Television and radio hardly reported the event.

Yet women had made themselves a subject of inquiry, challenge and examination. The Prime Minister, Yitschak Rabin, set up a committee to investigate the status of women.[1] Women were beginning to produce a counter-culture.

The Abortion Bill came up for first reading in February 1976. For this reading the two proposed Bills had been merged into one. The new Bill included the list of conditions and a newly formed approval clause. This proposed approval by a gynaecologist and either a general practitioner, a social worker or a public health nurse. The woman would have free choice and could make her own decision about whom she went to for approval. No established committee was set up. With this Bill the only women who would have difficulty in obtaining free abortion were those who, ironically, had been the most privileged beneficiaries before. They were middle-class, well set-up women with one or two children, who, previously, had used the facility illegally.

The Bill passed the first reading in the Knesset on 10 February 1976. In a half empty chamber only six women Members were present. Menachem Begin, leader of the right-wing Likud Party, had just returned from a trip abroad and disrupted the debate by walking about the chamber, shaking hands and drawing attention to himself. His behaviour was more reminiscent of a synagogue or market place than of a seat of government.[2] However, after a powerful speech by Chaika Grossman,[3] who presented the Bill, the motion was carried by nineteen, forty-six voting in favour and twenty-seven against. Geula Cohen, the only woman in the Likud alliance, voted against the motion. Shulamith Aloni was not present for the debate or the vote. After the first reading, the opponents of the Bill wanted it deferred indefinitely. However, this was fought and the Bill returned to committee for preparation of the second and third readings.

The women felt relieved and thought they could now relax a little as the Bill moved safely along. However, this illusion of success was soon shattered. After the Bill passed the first reading an open letter appeared in all the newspapers. It had been signed by five eminent doctors, members of the Secretariat of the Gynaecological Association of Israel, part of the Medical Histadruth, stating that they objected to the present Bill, because it granted too much freedom to women. They stated, too, that if it was enacted they would refuse to cooperate with it and refuse to perform abortions.[4]

On 23 June the national convention of the Society of Gynaecologists and Obstetricians was due to take place at the Tel Aviv Hilton. The women decided to form a group, break into the convention hall and demonstrate in front of the convention. They were angry at the letter and incensed at the financial situation regarding illegal abortions. The figure of illegal abortions annually in the country has been estimated at 80,000. More conservative estimates were 45,000. Prices for each abortion were in the range, 1,500 I£ to 3,500 I£. If an average figure of 2,000 I£ is used and the low estimate of 45,000 abortions is taken, it can be seen that 90,000,000 I£ per year in undeclared tax-free income was being distributed between several hundred gynaecologists in the country. (There are some six hundred gynaecologists and it is not known what proportion of them undertake illegal abortions on a regular basis.) Even if all were performing abortions it was about half a million Israeli pounds per year, each, in untaxed income.[5]

In all, eleven women, including Marcia, arrived at the Hilton Hotel in Tel Aviv during the convention, carrying placards under their clothes. As they arrived at the main entrance they discovered that their plan had been leaked and they were not allowed in. However, a woman who knew of their plans was already inside the building and led them straight into the hall by a side entrance. The point they were about to make was to draw the attention of the conference to the hypocracy of the doctors in opposing the Bill. They walked into the Hall, unrolling their placards, two women at a time, holding hands, shaking with fear. None, including Marcia, had ever undertaken such an event before. They were all very scared and had talked about their fears beforehand. As a result they had decided that as they were all frightened they would decide, in advance, who would start the shouting of slogans so that they would not all be waiting for someone else to begin. They started chanting as soon as they entered the hall and they repeated the same three slogans throughout. These were 'My body belongs to me,' 'Against "black" money' (this is the name given to tax evasion). 'Free choice, legal abortion.'

To the utter astonishment of the several hundred assembled gynaecologists they made their way to the podium chanting and waving their placards. They mounted the stage and stood in a line across it. As the line formed the gynaecologists, surprised and confused, absurdly started clapping their hands to the chanting. As planned, Marcia approached the chairman of the session (it was not until afterwards that she realized that he was one of the few gynaecologists who had consistently supported legalized abortion on demand) and asked to speak for ten or fifteen minutes. She said that when they had had their say they would leave quietly and the doctors could resume their meeting. He refused and she asked again, gently, while the women continued chanting in the background. Again he refused and she said that he was making a bad mistake and that he should allow them to speak. While these negotiations were going on the delegates in the body of the hall began to get up and go towards the stage trying to persuade the women to leave. Suddenly, three hotel security guards appeared and tried to push the women off the platform. The women returned the aggression of the security guards. Several photographers, invited by the feminists, were present taking pictures. They were pounced on by the security guards and the gynaecologists. A photographer was hit with his own flash gun by one of the gynaecologists. The women ran to help the photographer and a free-for-all ensued. At one point, one of the gynaecologists threw a heavy jug of water at Marcia dousing her.[6] The jug itself missed but fell with much force on the foot of one of the gynaecologists (a signatory of the letter), badly injuring his toe. The gynaecologists began throwing vases and glasses at the women. The women, tactically in the wrong, returned the fire. For about half-an-hour the fracas continued. Most of the gynaecologists were pinned against the three walls of the hall, some very angry, some trying to talk reasonably to the women in the midst of the mêlée. Throughout, the women did not stop chanting slogans. At a certain point, in an effort to cool the situation, the Chairman asked the delegates to leave. This they did slowly, at which the women began chanting 'Gynaecologists are afraid of women.' The women were then asked if they too would leave, but they refused, wishing to remain until the gynaecologists returned to listen to them. The police were called and informed them that they were under arrest; that they had trespassed on private property, that they had disturbed the peace etc., and requested the women to leave quietly with them. The women said that they would not as they were waiting for the doctors to return. The police then radioed for reinforcements and the women decided to use passive resistance when they were arrested. While waiting for the rest of the police and the paddy wagon to arrive, the eleven women sat down on the stage and prepared themselves for their ejection from the Hall. They began to soothe themselves and each other, consciously calmed down, picked up flowers that were strewn round, took a rose in each of their hands and gently waited to be removed.

The police arrived (they heard later that women police refused to join in the arrest) and were embarrassed at having to carry out prone, limp women. By this time radio reporters and the television cameras had arrived and were witnessing the scene of women being carried in an undignified way through the foyer of the re-splendent Hilton Hotel on the sea-front in Tel Aviv. As they left the building the women gave the liberation salute of the clenched fist.

Once in the paddy wagon, the women realized the importance of the whole operation and the success they had achieved. They were overjoyed and buoyant. En route to the police station they were surrounded by people at every traffic light they stopped at. Each time they chanted their slogans and held mini-demonstrations along the route to the police station, through the windows of the paddy wagon.

At the police station they were charged and released on bail. Although she had parliamentary immunity, Marcia insisted that she too be charged, but she was not asked for bail and could not resist further. Subsequently, she asked the Knesset to rescind her parliamentary immunity, but this was refused.

The 'Hilton Affair' as it came to be known, was probably the most important single event of the whole five years of feminist activity. For weeks afterwards the issue of abortion and feminism was constantly in the public eye. On radio and television the subject was discussed, dissected and analysed *ad infinitum*. Articles giving every point of view appeared in all the newspapers and magazines. Public forums were held by political parties, religious movements, universities, women's organizations. The Tel Aviv women spent all their time ensuring that the point of view of the feminists was put across. They wrote articles for publication, arranged interviews, and answered questions from each and every inquirer. Above all, discussion centred on the tactics used by the women and the value of those tactics. Only the Black Panthers had used similar devices to gain attention to their cause since the days of the British Mandate. The society thought it 'in bad taste'. For women, both inside and outside the Movement it was exhilarating. During the week, Marcia attended a symposium arranged by 'At' magazine (the leading women's magazine) on the whole question of civil disobedience and confrontation politics. But the women had shown their commitment to what they believed in and, most of all, demonstrated how seriously they took the abortion issue and with what earnestness they viewed their cause.

Following the 'Hilton Affair', Marcia raised in the Knesset for debate and not for statute, the issue of wife-beating. She had been exploring the subject for some time but had not previously raised it in public outside her Party. Inspired by Erin Pizzey's book *Scream Quietly or the Neighbours Will Hear*,[7] she and the feminists were interested in setting up hostels and half-way houses for battered wives and their children. Support had been forthcoming from WIZO, the Women's International Zionist Organisation, and this backing had encouraged Marcia to try and elicit support from Knesset members. Although she had become used to the backlash which her speeches often raised in the Knesset, she was nevertheless shocked by the response to this debate from the male members of the Knesset. They were furious at a public debate on the subject, shouting, arguing and vilifying her. 'What if the woman deserves it,' they screamed, and 'What about men who are beaten by their wives? Are you advocating similar measures for them?' There was uproar in the House. Women Knesset Members were insulted and outraged by this reaction. For the first time they unanimously joined together and backed Marcia. And then the letters came in. To Marcia Freedman in the Knesset, all kinds of women, from all over the country wrote of their experiences at the hands of brutish, bullying husbands and fathers, and expressed their gratitude that the matter was at last being aired.

In terms of political development the 'Hilton Affair' and the outspokenness on the wife-battering issue crystalized the feminists as a radical, progressive movement offering one of the few positive alternatives to the existing society. The radical left had been dormant for some time, afraid, probably, of all the things the women had been afraid of for generations. The women were no longer afraid, had shown integrity, militancy, bravery and leadership on issues which were fundamental, on a human level, to the life of the country for men and women alike.

When the Women's Movement started some five years previously, it had been tentative, exploratory, timid, unsure of itself. 'It wasn't needed in Israel,' people had said everywhere. 'Maybe in the United States, but here women have equality, it is built into the Declaration of Independence.' By 1976 the feminists had opened up a whole world of institutionalized oppression, public and private tyranny and intimidation. They were on their way to a realization of their aims. Maybe they were also building a Movement of Liberation.

20. The Future

In the first five years of its life the Movement had tipped the values and standards of the State upside down and had brought to the forefront of people's minds ideas and thoughts concerning feelings, needs and emotional satisfactions. Homosexuality, prostitution, grief, fear, anguish, women themselves, had become, because of the outspokenness of a few brave women and because women in general had found a voice, subjects of prime importance. Where once the very existence of these matters had been totally denied (even amongst the 'avant-garde', progressive talk had centred on external affairs: better relations with the Arabs, the future of Zionism, Jewish nationalism), they became more open, looser issues, discussed, dissected and argued. During her time as leader of the Movement, Marcia Freedman had instigated discussion on personal issues wherever and whenever she could. For six years or so she had been a tireless exponent of feminism and humanism and had been outspoken in her support of both. Other women, too, taking her lead, had come from the shadows to speak out, vociferously.

Throughout 1976 and 1977 the women continued their activities. In June 1976 Marcia Freedman and another Israeli delegate attended the International Tribunal on Crimes Against Women, in Brussels. All the major cities had branches of the Movement – Haifa, Jerusalem, Tel Aviv and Beersheva and by November 1977 there were 1,000 women on the Movement's mailing list.[1]

Towards the end of 1976 the Movement decided to establish a Women's Party which would put up a candidate to fight the coming election, planned for May 1977. Marcia Freedman decided not to stand for re-election and as existing parties are financed by the State, each MK has a budget for political purposes. Marcia

Freedman used her government grant of about half-a-million Israeli pounds (£20,000) to promote a Women's Party.

The Party received between 5,000 and 6,000 votes in the election
– not enough to gain a seat in the Knesset. The candidate was
almost unknown and lacked Marcia Freedman's charisma. The
Party had been hastily formed, the candidate hastily chosen and
the whole political climate of the country had shifted away from
the Labour Party to the right-wing Likud Party of which Menachem Begin was the leader.

As she finally dropped out of national politics, Marcia Freedman started to pursue the idea of setting up a new kind of
Women's Centre. This was to provide for rape-crisis projects, abortion referral, birth control counselling and a refuge for battered
wives. The Centre opened in Haifa on 1 November 1977 and on 21
November 1977 Marcia Freedman wrote: 'The first serious run-
away has come to stay, with five little kids and a body covered
with scars ... The general response to our existence has been
serious and warm – something none of us are used to and that
wouldn't have happened earlier.'[2]

The election of May 1977 brought the first dramatic change of
government since 1948. Menachem Begin became Prime Minister,
heralding an alliance with the National Religious Party. On an
international level this brought about détente between Israel and
Egypt and a speech delivered by Anwar Sadat in the Knesset in
November 1977. Afterwards came the peace talks, the Camp
David summit[3] and the Nobel Peace Prize for Sadat and Begin.[4]

At home the change in the political leadership was viewed with
anxiety and concern by the feminists. By the autumn of 1977 the
Abortion Law was already under attack by the Begin Government
and the alliance with the Religious Bloc was worrying, since opposition to abortion reform had always come from religious,
nationalistic and medical circles. Much of the women's activity
focused on the setting up of refuges, as other groups began to look
at the pioneering development in Haifa. At a general meeting held
after the election it was decided not to reconstitute the parliamentary party.

But, in the years before, a new era for women had clearly been born so that nothing would ever be the same again. 'Women here live like American women in the 50s. Nevertheless, I think that things are moving towards a woman's awareness of our exploitation and I am confident in the future of the Movement in this country,' said Marcia Freedman in an interview with Manuela Lombardo.[5]

The form which the Women's Movement of Israel will take as it moves into the 1980s is open to discussion, for it is not yet clear how the new Government, if it remains, will influence events in relation to women nor how subtly their position will be endangered. That the feminists set a new moral tone, is, to those who knew the Movement throughout the period under discussion, unquestionable. Whether that new morality can continue to flourish or whether it will have to go underground to is an issue for the feminists and their historians.

Feminism is established in Israel; so is the Abortion Law, the continuing dialogue on prostitution, the feminist groups throughout the country spreading information, knowledge and strength, the concern about rape and the Women's Centre, the first of many. In January 1978 Marcia Freedman wrote:

> The refuge and related projects are almost too successful at the moment. There are fourteen women and as many children already terribly overcrowded ... during the last few weeks women have been coming at the rate of two a week and each comes to stay for a couple of months ... But what's happening is that women come and can't believe what they find ... 'It's ideal' they all say, because no one is telling them what to do, offering help with strings attached, limiting their freedom and they are shocked and surprised – and begin to grow and get strong in the atmosphere. What really happens is that they become gradually, and, without exception, activists. And these are poor women with lots of kids and no education – the ones who've been fucked over all their lives. It's beautiful to see. So beautiful that I know we'll solve the problems.[6]

Although she was writing about the new Women's Centre, Marcia Freedman's vision may also be true, both for the Movement and for all Israeli women.

Notes

INTRODUCTION
1. *Portnoy's Complaint*, Philip Roth, Jonathan Cape, 1969.

1. FROM SHTETL TO YISHUV
1. Mark Zborowski and Elizabeth Herzog, *Life is with People*, Schocken Books, U.S.A., 1970, p. 130.
2. Rabbi Dr Isadore Epstein, *Judaism, a Historical Perspective*, Penguin Books, 1959, p. 168.
3. See Jacob Frumkin, Gregor Aronson and Alexis Goldenweiser, *Russian Jewry*, 1860–1917, pp. 100–101. Thomas Yoseloff, U.S.A. 1966.
4. See Salo Baron, *The Russian Jews under Czars and Soviets*, Macmillan, 1964, p. 19.
5. Louis Greenberg, *The Jews in Russia: Struggle for Emancipation*, Yale University Press, New Haven and London, 2 vols., 1944 and 1951, pp. 30–31.
6. The Romanoffs were the Russian ruling dynasty from the accession of Michael in 1613 until the overthrow of the dynasty, headed at that time by Nicholas II, in 1917.
7. Frumkin, Aronson and Goldenweiser, op. cit., pp. 101–2.
8. The May Laws were a series of 'temporary laws' applying to Jews confirmed by Tsar Alexander III in May 1882 and repealed in March 1917 by the revolutionary provisional government. These 'temporary regulations' stated:
   a. Jews are forbidden to settle outside the towns and townlets.
   b. Deeds of sale and lease of real estate in the name of Jews outside the towns or townlets are cancelled and
   c. Jews are prohibited from trading on Sundays and Christian holidays.
   [Bearing in mind that their own Sabbath fell on Saturdays when they would have refrained from trading and that they observed their own religious holidays, this new restriction severely curtailed their ability to earn a living.]
9. Louis Golding, *The Jewish Problem*, Penguin Books, 1938, p. 96.

10. Irving Howe, *The Immigrant Jews of New York*, Routledge & Kegan Paul, 1976, p. 11.
11. For more on this aspect of Jewish life see Irving Howe, op. cit.
12. Zborowski and Herzog, op. cit., pp. 128–9.
13. ibid., p. 129.
14. ibid., p. 136.
15. S. Diamond, 'Kibbutz and Shtetl: the history of an idea', *Social Problems*, Vol. 2, No. 2, Autumn, 1957, published by the Society for the Study of Social Problems, U.S.A., p. 79.
16. Zborowski and Herzog, op. cit., p. 130.
17. ibid., pp. 132–3.
18. S. Diamond, op. cit., p. 79.
19. Zborowski and Herzog, op. cit., p. 150.
20. ibid., p. 132.
21. This aspect of Jewish life is poignantly demonstrated by Jewish novelists of the time and is graphically described also by the present-day writer Isaac Bashevis Singer in his saga, *The Manor*, published by Penguin Books, 1975. Chekhov also alludes to it in his play *The Cherry Orchard*.
22. St Petersburg and Moscow.
23. Salo Baron, op. cit., p. 81.
24. L. Shapiro, *The Role of Jews in the Russian Revolutionary Movement*, Slavonic and East European Review, Vol. XL, 1961–2, no. 94, p. 149.
25. Louis Golding, op. cit., p. 97.
26. Salo Baron, op. cit., p. 87.
27. Louis Greenberg, op. cit., p. 147.
28. ibid., p. 149.
29. My brackets.
30. J. L. Talmon, *Israel among the Nations*, Weidenfeld & Nicolson 1972, p. 26.
31. David Vital, *The Origins of Zionism*, Oxford University Press, 1975, p. 313.
32. ibid., p. 313.
33. L. Shapiro, op. cit., p 148.
34. This earlier movement which started in the 1880s was called Hibbat Zion (Love of Zion).
35. The Zionist movements in Eastern Europe had youth movements which sent groups to Palestine and it was from these youth movements that many of the young settlers came.
36. Melvin Spiro, *Kibbutz – Venture in Utopia*. First published by Harvard University Press, 1956, p. 111.

37. *The Manor* and *The Estate.*
38. Manya Wilbushewitch Shochat (1881–1961), one of the leaders of the Hashomer group (referred to in Chapter 2, pp. 34–5) and an early pioneer.
39. Amos Elon, *The Israelis – Founders and Sons*, first published by Weidenfeld & Nicolson, 1971, p. 191.
40. Louis Greenberg, op. cit., p. 154.
41. ibid., p. 142.
42. Dr S. Rolbant, *Mapia – Labour Party of Israel*, Poale Zion, London, 1949, p. 8.
43. Walter Laqueur, *A History of Zionism*, Weidenfeld & Nicolson, 1972, p. 280.
44. The various important immigration waves are discussed in Chapter 3.
45. Walter Laqueur, op. cit., p. 281.
46. The age Elon attributes to Manya Shochat on her first visit to Palestine in 1914 does not agree with my researches (see note 38). However, since birth records of that time were not very accurate it would be difficult to gauge her correct age on arrival in Palestine.
47. Amos Elon, op. cit., p. 192.
48. The Hermitage Library was in St Petersburg.
49. Amos Elon, op. cit., p. 24.

2. FIRST, SECOND AND THIRD ALIYAH

1. From *The Plough Woman, Records of the Pioneer Women of Palestine*, edited by Rachel Katzenelson-Rubashow, Nicholas L. Brown Inc. New York, 1932, p. 35.
2. Harry Viteles, *A History of the Cooperative Movement in Israel*, Book Two, *The Evolution of the Kibbutz Movement*, Valentine Michell, 1967, p. 35.
3. David Ben Gurion, *Israel, a personal history*, Funk & Wagnalls Inc., U.S.A., 1971, p. 36.
4. Amos Elon, op. cit., p. 40.
5. See Vital, op. cit., p. 357.
6. 1626–76. The central figure of Shabataiism, the largest and most momentous messianic movement in Jewish history subsequent to the destruction of The Temple (586 B.C.).
7. Vital, op. cit., p. 345.
8. Pseudonym for Asher Hirsch Ginsberg (1856–1927). Hebrew

essayist in Palestine, thinker and leader of Hibbat Zion movement.

9. Ahad Ha'am, *The Jewish State and the Jewish Problem*, published in The Zionist Idea, by Arthur Hertzberg, Doubleday & Co., Inc. and Herzl Press, New York, (no date), p. 263.

10. Throughout Part 1 of this book, the word 'Palestinian' refers to the Jewish settlers in Palestine before the creation of the State of Israel.

11. Walter Laqueur, op. cit., p. 284.

12. 1849–1923. Co-founder of the World Zionist Organization.

13. Walter Laqueur, op. cit., p. 288.

14. 1864–1943, German sociologist and economist, an initiator of cooperative agriculture in Palestine.

15. From the article 'History of the Working Women in Israel' in *Features of Israel*, No 24, March 1975, Tel Aviv, p. 7.

16. From *The Plough Woman*, op. cit., p. 57.

17. Melvin Spiro, op. cit., p. 222.

18. *The Plough Woman*, op. cit., p. 57.

19. There may be some puzzlement over the use of the term 'colonist'. The Jewish labour movement in Palestine began only in the twentieth century; Jewish colonization before that time was almost exclusively of the 'planter' type. The struggle of the Jewish land-worker to find a place for himself in the agricultural economy ran up against the opposition of the old individualist planters who had built their system on the use of cheap, exploited and unorganized Arab labour. In the twentieth century the two types of Jewish colonization went on side by side, with the worker type (representing also a specific social idealism cast in specific forms) on the increase. The gradual infiltration of Jewish labour into Jewish colonies is an important chapter in the integration of the society.

20. Izhak Ben Zvi, 1884–1963, second president of Israel, 1952–62, founder and leader of Zionist–Socialism.

21. David Ben Gurion, 1886–1973, Israeli Statesman, first Prime Minister and Defence Minister of Israel.

22. This was the philosophy held by many of the early settlers that labour for its own sake was an end in itself and it was on this principle that they conducted their lives.

23. Amos Elon, op. cit., p. 123.

24. ibid., p. 124.

25. Arthur Koestler, *Promise and Fulfilment, Palestine 1917–1949*, Macmillan, 1949, p. 37.

26. Amos Perlmutter, *Military and Politics in Israel, Nation-building and Role Expansion*, Frank Cass & Co., Ltd., 1969, p. 5.
27. ibid., p. 5.
28. ibid., p. 5.
29. ibid., pp. 5–6.
30. Arthur Koestler, op. cit., p. 67.
31. 1894–1940. Labour leader in Palestine; housing complex Ramat Remes near Haifa, named in his honour.
32. Moshe Sharett, 1894–1965, Israeli statesman and Zionist leader.
33. Labour leader in Palestine, active in Histadrut and Haganah.
34. 1886–   Hebrew writer, received the Israel Prize, 1965.
35. 1889–   Third President of Israel.
36. Walter Laqueur, op. cit., p. 311.
37. Lionel Tiger and Joseph Shepher, *Women in the Kibbutz*, Harcourt Brace Johanovitch, New York, 1975; and Penguin Books, Harmondsworth, 1977, p. 79.
38. Melvin Spiro, op. cit., p. 111.
39. Joseph Baratz, *Degania – the Story of Palestine's First Collective Settlement*, Palestine Pioneer Library, 1931, p. 28.
40. *The Plough Woman*, op. cit., p. 182.
41. Bruno Bettelheim, *Children of the Dream*, Paladin, 1971, p. 40.
42. There were 500,000 Arabs and 85,000 Jews in Palestine in the year 1914. (Source: Howard M. Sacher, *A History of Israel from the Rise of Zionism to our Time*, Alfred A. Knopf, U.S.A., 1976, p. 87.)
43. 1887–1944, leader of the Zionist Labour Movement.
44. Walter Laqueur, op. cit., p. 267.
45. David Ben Gurion, op. cit., p. 41.
46. ibid., p. 42.
47. A movement which tried to base itself in the Jewish proletariat and whose ideology consisted of a combination of Zionism and Socialism.
48. Hapoel Hatzair – Young Workers' Party. A movement based on a principle of 'conquest of labour'. More an ideological society than a political movement, it disdained to match the Poale Zion in organized activities or propaganda.
49. Jews of Yemen. Immigration of Jews from the Yemen began in 1882 at the same time as the first Aliyah from Russia. They dominated the building trades, working in quarries as stone cutters and as masons, construction labourers and plasterers as well as in every craft where work was available. At the end of World War I there were 4,500 Yemenite Jews in the country.

50. Walter Laqueur, op. cit., p. 287.
51. Yonina Talmon, *Family and Community in the Kibbutz*, Harvard University Press, U.S.A. 1972, p. 7.
52. Walter Laqueur, op. cit., p. 322.
53. The first *moshav ovedim* in Palestine, founded in 1921 in the Western Jezreel valley by veteran pioneers of the Second Aliyah.
54. Naava Eisin, *The Working Women of Israel*, Histadrut – General Federation of Labour, Israel, 1975, p. 15.
55. *The Plough Woman*, op. cit., p. 140.
56. Tiger and Shepher, op. cit., p. 85.
57. These were pioneers who formed themselves into groups to undertake the hard, manual work of clearing the ground, draining swamps, building kibbutzim.
58. Amos Elon, op. cit., pp. 145–6.
59. Golda Meir, *My Life*, Weidenfeld & Nicolson, 1975, p. 67.
60. ibid., p. 69.

3. THE BIRTH OF CHAUVINISM

1. Walter Laqueur, op. cit., p. 308.
2. Figures taken from *Features of Israel*, op. cit., p. 9.
3. Joseph Sprinzak (1885–1959), Labour leader and first speaker of the Knesset (1949–59).
4. The Histadrut is the largest labour union and largest voluntary organization in Israel. In 1969 it had a membership of 1,038,653.
5. Full name: Union of Zionist Revisionism, abbreviated Hebrew name: *Ha-Zohar*. Movement of nationalist political Zionists formed and led by Vladimir Jabotinsky. In the late 1920s and 1930s the Revisionists became the principal Zionist opposition party to Chaim Weizmann's leadership and to the methods and policy of the World Zionist Organisation.
6. Naava Eisin, op. cit., p. 18.
7. International non-government body centred in Jerusalem, formalized in August 1828. It is the executive and representative of the World Zionist Organisation and aims to assist and encourage Jews throughout the world to help in the development and settlement of Israel.
8. Irgun Zvai Leumi (I.Z.L.), literally, National Military Organisation, the largest of the Jewish underground dissident movements was formed in 1931.
9. Amos Perlmutter, op. cit., p. 25.
10. ibid., p. 29.

11. ibid., p. 29.
12. Palmach – (Hebrew: *Plugot Machatz* – shock companies) the striking arm of the Haganah.
13. Yigal Allon, *Shield of David, the Story of Israel's Armed Forces*, Weidenfeld & Nicolson, London, 1970, p. 128.
14. Amos Perlmutter, op. cit., p. ix.
15. During my researches in Israel I spoke to several women who, clearly, had played an important part in the Haganah and the I.Z.L. However, it was not possible to trace any recorded information about them.
16. 1949–51.
17. Religious Zionist Movement founded in 1902.
18. This was the first attempt by the Jews of Palestine at democratic self-government. Elections for the First National Assembly took place in April 1920. Some 20,000 persons, more than 70 per cent of all registered Jewish voters took part in the ballot. The newly elected National Assembly opened formally in Jerusalem in October 1920. In general its power remained minimal and its influence little. (For more on this see Sacher, op. cit.)
19. Ultra-religious party.
20. David Ben Gurion, op. cit., p. 375.
21. The name given to the women's corps, in Hebrew meaning 'charm'. As an acrostic the word symbolizes 'need'.
22. Tom Bowden, *Army in the Service of the State*, University Publishing projects, Tel Aviv, 1976, pp. 98–9.

4. INDEPENDENCE FOR WHOM?

1. Moshe Lissak, *Social Mobility in Israel Society*, Israel University Press, Jerusalem, 1969, p. viii.
2. Sephardim (Sing: Sephardi) descendants of Jews who lived in Spain and Portugal before their expulsion in 1492. When the Inquisition was established a decree of expulsion was issued (in March 1492) against all those Jews who refused to accept Christianity and this edict officially remained in force until 1968. Some accepted conversion others, approximately 250,000, moved away to North Africa, Italy and Turkey where they were welcomed by Sultan Bayezid II. Jews of Portugal left about a century later and settled mainly in Holland.
3. Amos Elon, op. cit., p. 302.
4. Avraham · Avihai, *Ben-Gurion, State Builder, Principles and*

Pragmatism, 1948–1963, Israel University Press, Jerusalem, 1974, p. 124.

5. This story was told to me by an Israeli feminist, herself researching feminist developments among the early pioneers.

6. Israel labour leader, Member of Knesset from 1949, Deputy Speaker, 1955–61.

7. All the information relating to the Female Labour Law of 1954 is taken from *The Working Women of Israel*, by Naava Eisin, op. cit.

8. Tova Sanhedrin was that Member of Knesset for fourteen years and the Deputy Speaker for ten. She was always conscious and sure of the role women should play in the society. Within the confines of religion she wanted women to achieve positions of significance and independence, thereby earning and gaining respect. With little help from her male colleagues, Tova Sanhedrin and the other women of Hapoel Hamizrachi (the Religious Workers Party) continued with their fight to help religious women gain status inside and outside parliament.

5. ORIENTAL, ARAB AND DRUSE WOMEN

1. Avraham Avihai, op. cit., p. 125.

2. Judah Matras, *Social Change in Israel*, Aldine Publishing Co., Chicago, 1965, p. 75, Table 2.15.

3. Moshe Lissak, op. cit., p. ix.

4. Dov Weintraub and associates, *Immigration and Social Change. Agricultural settlement of new immigrants in Israel*, Manchester University Press, Manchester, U.K., 1971, p. 10.

5. ibid., p. 125.

6. Information about the Druse people was hard to find. Living mainly in the northern part of Israel they lead private, traditional lives. However, in recent years the development of industry has integrated them more into the lifestyle of the country. Their children sometimes attend state schools in near-by towns with Jewish and Arab children. There are about 30,000 Druse people in Israel.

7. Sacher writes: 'When the fighting ended, (in 1948) an estimated 156,000 Arabs remained within Israel's borders, a number that would nearly quadruple in subsequent years. They continued to make their homes essentially in a hundred towns and villages of their own, and in five mixed towns – Acre, Haifa, Jaffa, Ramla and Jerusalem – with large Jewish majorities. Approximately 60 per cent of the Arab population lived in the Galilee, another 20 per cent in the 'little triangle' of farm villages abutting the Jordanian frontier; while two smaller enclaves, each encompassing about 7

per cent of the Arab population, remained in the Haifa area and in the Negev. All these Arab population centres, in any case, were quite near Israel's land borders, and it was this very proximity to nations intent upon the destruction of the Jewish State that conditioned and qualified many of Israel's pre-war assurances of equal citizenship,' op. cit., pp. 382–3.

8. Noah Lucas, *The Modern History of Israel*, Weidenfeld & Nicolson, London, 1974, pp. 355–6.
9. Sabri Jiryis, 'The Arabs in Israel', *Monthly Review Press*, New York and London, undated, p. 205.
10. Features of Israel, op. cit., p. 50.
11. Sabri Jiryis, op. cit., p. 205.
12. Much money from the World Zionist Organisation has, historically, been channelled through the Jewish Agency and therefore has only found its way to projects for the Jewish community. For a detailed account of the work of the Jewish Agency see Sacher, op. cit.
13. Noah Lucas, op. cit., p. 355.
14. Howard M. Sacher, op. cit., pp. 537–8.
15. Arabs are not called into the I.D.F. Druse men serve in some sections, most especially in the border police.
16. These were the years from the establishment of the State until the June War of 1967, when the Arabs were completely cut off from their Arab neighbours. With the new borders, after 1967, the situation changed somewhat.
17. Howard M. Sacher, op. cit., p. 706.
18. Figures taken from An'am Zuabi, *The Arab Woman 'Twixt Tradition and Progress*, Features of Israel, op. cit., p. 55.
19. ibid., p. 56.
20. ibid., p. 55.

6. DAYAN, SINAI AND THE GROWTH OF MACHISMO

1. The fictitious name given by Spiro to the kibbutz which he researched in the book already cited.
2. Spiro, op. cit., p. 236.
3. Shabtai Teveth, *Moshe Dayan*, Weidenfeld & Nicolson, London and Jerusalem, 1972, p. 147.
4. Noah Lucas, op. cit., p. 356.
5. Abbreviation for Mifleget Poale Eretz Israel (Israel's Labour Party) formed when Hapoel Hatzair united with Ahdut Ha-Avoda in 1929. It is social democratic in its orientation.

6. Avraham Avihai, op. cit., pp. 260–61.

7. David Ben Gurion, op. cit., p. 8.

8. Samuel Rolbant, *The Israeli Soldier – Profile of an Army*, Thomas Yoseloff, U.S.A, 1970, p. 9.

9. Tom Bowden, op. cit., p. 10.

10. Joseph W. Eaton in collaboration with Michael Chen, *Influencing the Youth Culture, A study of Youth Organisation in Israel*, Sage Publications, 1970, U.S.A., p. 90.

11. Shabtai Teveth, op. cit., p. 223.

12. Amos Perlmutter, op. cit., p. 75.

13. Also known as 'Operation Kadesh', it took place from 29 October to 5 November 1956, between Egypt and Israel.

14. Edward Luttwak and Dan Horowitz, *The Israeli Army*, Allen Lane, 1975, p. 164.

15. For more on this subject see, Erskine B. Childers, *The Road to Suez*, MacGibbon & Kee, 1962; Randolph Churchill, *The Rise and Fall of Sir Anthony Eden*, MacGibbon & Kee, 1959; Moshe Dayan, *Diary of the Sinai Campaign*, Har-Row, U.S.A., 1965; Edgar O'Ballance, *The Sinai Campaign*, Faber & Faber, 1959.

16. Noah Lucas, op. cit., p. 390.

17. The Mitla and Gidi passes were strategic points in the 1956, 1967 and 1973 wars. Geographically, they commanded the only serviceable route traversing Sinai from north to south, opening passage to and from the Canal and integral Egypt.

18. Assaf Simhoni was appointed commander of southern command in the autumn of 1956. On 29 October he commanded the I.D.F. in the Sinai Campaign receiving the surrender of the Egyptian governor of the Gaza Strip; he died in a plane crash shortly after the campaign and was posthumously promoted to major-general.

19. Shabtai Teveth, op. cit., p. 269.

20. Luttwak and Horowitz, op. cit., p. 163.

21. Dayan wears a black eye-patch over his left eye as a result of being wounded in 1941 when serving in the Haganah.

22. Ben Gurion's phrase.

23. Shimon Peres – politician. Director-general of Defence Ministry from 1953. Deputy Minister of Defence from 1959–65.

24. Amos Perlmutter, op. cit., p. 93.

25. Amos Elon, op. cit., p. 321.

26. The headquarters of the Tammany, a political organization founded in Manhattan, New York, U.S.A., after the War of American Independence. It exercised great influence over the Democratic Party in New York. It became notorious for corruption in the

nineteenth century, notably 1865 to 1867 when, under Tweed, it gained control of New York and defrauded it of many millions of dollars. The organization declined in the 1930s. The name comes from a seventeenth century Delaware Indian Chief, Tamanend.

27. Reuben Slonim, *Both Sides Now, a twenty-five year encounter with Arabs and Israelis,* Clarke Irwin & Co., Ltd, Canada, 1972, p. 94.

28. Initiated by the U.S. Government in 1955 for the utilization of the Jordan and Yarmuk rivers by dividing them among Israel, Syria, Lebanon and the Kingdom of Jordan but the Arab League rejected the plan.

29. An area comprising those southern parts of Israel which are characterized by a totally arid desert climate. It is an area exceeding 12,000 sq kilometres and, on the map is described as an inverted triangle with an apex directed to Eilat in the south.

30. Michael Brecher, *The Foreign Policy System of Israel, Settings, Images, Process,* Oxford University Press, London, 1972, p. 44.

31. Joseph W. Eaton, op. cit., p. 162.

32. Samuel Rolbant, op. cit., p. 90.

33. Noah Lucas, op. cit., 422–3.

34. ibid.

35. Samuel Rolbant, p. 298.

36. Amos Elon, op. cit., p. 243.

7. THE SIX-DAY WAR AND THE INFLUENCE OF THE UNITED STATES

1. Abba Eban, *My Country, the story of Modern Israel,* Weidenfeld & Nicolson, 1974, p. 246.

2. Chaim Herzog, *The War of Atonement,* Weidenfeld & Nicolson, 1975, p. 2.

3. Samuel Rolbant, op. cit., p. 141.

4. Moshe Davis (ed.), *The Yom Kippur War, Israel and the Jewish People,* Arno Press, U.S.A., 1974, p. 55.

5. Noah Lucas, op. cit., p. 423.

6. City of Negev. Market centre of the Negev Bedouin. Has Jewish population of around 100,000. It is the capital of Israel's Southern district.

7. Amos Elon, op. cit., p. 234.

8. In Hebrew: *Kotel Ma'aravi.* Before 1967 known as the Wailing Wall. It is the most sacred spot for the male religious Jews of Israel and the Diaspora, being the only remains of the walls of the Second Temple.

9. This information is based on talks I had in London with women wishing to emigrate and with immigration officials of the Jewish Agency in London.

8. THE ERA OF THE RUSSIAN IMMIGRANT

1. Howard M. Sacher, op. cit., p. 737.
2. Michael Brecher, op. cit., p. 306.
3. David Ben Gurion, op. cit., p. 839.
4. Related to me by several social workers in the field.

9. BOOM YEARS 1971 TO 1973

1. Howard M. Sacher, op. cit., p. 746.
2. ibid., p. 746.
3. Asher Arian, *The Elections in Israel – 1973*, Jerusalem Academic Press, 1975, p. 127.
4. Howard M. Sacher, op. cit., p. 833.
5. Asher Arian, op. cit., p. 11.

10. WOMEN IN THE YOM KIPPUR WAR

1. Extract from 'The Working Women of Israel', published by the Women Workers Council and reprinted in 'Features of Israel', 1975.
2. From Kippur, an account of Israel's October 1973 war, by seven of the country's columnists and correspondents, Special Edition Publishers, Israel, 1973, p. 2.
3. Howard M. Sacher, op. cit., pp. 786–7.
4. ibid., p. 787.
5. Taken from information sheets circulated by the Women's Movement and from Nilachem, the journal of the Women's Movement.
6. Luttwak and Horowitz, op. cit., p. 79–80.

11. THE 1973 ELECTION – ISRAEL REASSESSES

1. Arian, op. cit., p. 9.
2. ibid., p. 12.
3. A former commander of the paratroopers.
4. Formerly Chief of Air Force and then Chief of Army Operations.
5. Member of Knesset 1973–7.

12. THE START OF THE WOMEN'S MOVEMENT

1. *Jerusalem Post*, Friday 4 February 1972.
2. For more on this see chapter 14 and for general reading on the subject see *Red Rag, A Magazine of Women's Liberation*, No. 11.
3. The Women's International Zionist Organisation referred to them as 'a drop in the ocean'. *Jerusalem Post*, Friday 2 January 1972.
4. See 'The Status of the Woman in Israel', Shulamith Aloni, from *Judaism, A Quarterly Journal of Jewish Life and Thought*, Vol. 22, No. 2, Spring Issue, 1973.

13. CONSCIOUSNESS-RAISING

1. For a long account of this see Leslie Hazelton, *Israeli Women – The Reality behind the Myths*, Simon & Schuster, New York, U.S.A., 1977.
2. Golda Meir, op. cit., p. 89.
3. The second-class status of women at that time was observed rather than documented, but as the Movement grew the women collected the facts which pin-pointed the discrimination.
4. These observations were confirmed in discussions with women in and out of the Women's Movement and are also referred to by Leslie Hazelton, op. cit.
5. (See p. 108).

14. THE SPREAD OF FEMINISM TO JERUSALEM AND TEL AVIV

1. Malka Maon, *Socialization for Fulfilling Sex Roles in Israel's State Schools* (in Hebrew), M.A. thesis at the University of Haifa.
2. 12 January 1973.
3. The Civil Rights Movement Party came into existence hurriedly before the 1973 elections. The Women's Movement was one of its original constituents.
4. At the time several of the Tel Aviv feminists were personal friends of Aloni.

15. FEMINISM AFTER THE OCTOBER WAR

1. Now Dean of Students at Bezalel Art Institute in Jerusalem and the 1977 Feminist Party Parliamentary Candidate.
2. *Yediot Acharonot*, 10 July 1974.
3. ibid.
4. 21 May 1974.
5. *Ma'ariv*, 23 May 1974.

16. ABORTION

1. Leslie Hazelton, op. cit., p. 81.

17. PROSTITUTION

1. The committee's findings were formally accepted by the Knesset in August 1978. For a report on this see the *Guardian*, 5 September 1978.
2. 23 May 1974.

18. 1975 – THE YEAR OF CHALLENGE

1. Meir, op. cit., p. 308.
2. Elon, op. cit., p. 341.
3. For a people whose lives have been dominated by death and grief, little research has been done on the subject, but a paper entitled 'Socio-cultural expressions and implications of Death, Mourning and Bereavement in Israel arising out of a War Situation', published in Israel Annals of Psychiatry and Related Disciplines, Vol. XI, No. 3, 1973, gives an interesting and useful view.

19. DEMONSTRATIONS AND THE 'HILTON AFFAIR'

1. *Jerusalem Post Weekly*, 6 January 1976.
2. My own personal observations.
3. Labour Party Knesset Member.
4. See *The Proceedings of the International Tribunal on Crimes Against Women*, compiled and edited by Diane E. H. Russell and Nicole Van de Ven, published by Les Femmes, U.S.A, 1976, p. 24.
5. Figures supplied by the Women's Movement.
6. *Jerusalem Post Weekly*, 29 June 1976.
7. Published by Penguin Books.

20. THE FUTURE

1. Interview with Marcia Freedman, *Spare Rib*, Issue 64, November 1977.
2. In correspondence with the writer.
3. September 1978.
4. October 1978.
5. *Spare Rib*, op. cit.
6. In correspondence with the writer.

Glossary

Aliyah:	(Plu. *Aliyot.*) The coming of the Jews to Palestine for permanent residence. From the Hebrew verb – *La'ahlot* – to go up.
Ashkenazi:	German, West-Central and East-European Jews.
Besmidresh:	House of study often attached to or serving as a synagogue. Also spelt *Bet-hamidrash*.
Barmitzvah:	(Plu. *Barmitzvot.*) The ceremony of manhood celebrated by Jewish boys on their thirteenth birthday. Also spelt *Bar Mitzvah*.
Chalutzim:	Comrades.
Chanukah:	The festival of lights held in December.
Chutzpah:	Vast impudence, excess of gall.
Golah:	Hebrew, meaning exile. Also known as *Galut*.
Haganah:	The underground military organization of the Yishuv in Palestine from 1920–48.
Halacha:	Ancient rabbinical laws which still govern marriage and divorce in Israel.
Hashomer:	Watchman.
Histadrut:	The General Federation of Labour.
Kheyder:	School for teaching children Jewish religious observance. Also spelt *Heder* or *Cheder*.
Kibbutz:	(Plu. *Kibbutzim.*) Collective or communal settlement based primarily on agriculture, in recent years diversifying into industry as well.
Knesset:	The Parliament of Israel consisting of a 120 member single chamber. The constituent Assembly met for the first time on 14 February 1949.
Mezuzah:	A small roll of parchment upon which has been flawlessly copied out the Jewish profession of faith

(*Shema*) and the additional biblical verses pertaining to the love of God, loyalty to His commandments and His recompense for fidelity. It is frequently encased in a decorated box of silver or wood but mostly in one of brass or glass and according to injunction in the verses of Deuteronomy VI, 9 and XI, 20, supplemented by the talmudic tractate Mezuzah is affixed to the entrance door of the house and to the doorposts of each room on the right side of the entrance.

Moshav Ovedim: (Plu. *Moshavim Ovedim*.) Agricultural village in Israel whose inhabitants possess individual homes and holdings but cooperate in the purchase of equipment, sale of produce, mutual aid, etc.

Reb: Yiddish form of Rabbi, applied generally to a teacher or hasidic rabbi. (Hasidism – main form of religious observance of Jews in Central and Eastern Europe at that time.)

Sheshbesh: Arabic for Backgammon.

Shtetl: Yiddish name given to the small towns in the Pale of Settlement inhabited by the Jews. From the German 'Stadt' – a little town.

Synagogue: Jewish religious place of worship.

Talmudic: Appertaining to the Talmud which is a compendium of discussions on the Mishnah by generations of scholars and jurists in many academies over a period of several centuries. (*Mishnah:* earliest codification of Jewish Oral Law.)

Tefillin: Phylacteries.

Torah: The generic name for the whole teaching of the Jewish law.

Vattikim: Hebrew word for old-time pioneers. Literal translation from the Hebrew – Old Ones. *Vattik* is masc. sing. *Vattika* is fem. sing.

Yeshiva: (Plu. *Yeshivot*.) Jewish traditional academy devoted primarily to study of the Rabbinic literature.

Yiddish: Vernacular of the Jews of Eastern Europe. Originally based on medieval German but later enlarged by the addition of truncated and mis-pronounced Hebrew.

Yishuv: The Jewish community of Palestine in the pre-State period. The pre-Zionist community is generally designated the 'old Yishuv' and the community evolving from 1880, the 'new Yishuv'.

Zahal: Initial of *Zva Haganah le'Israel*. The Israel Defence Forces.

Index

A selection of books published by Penguin is listed on the following pages.

For a complete list of books available from Penguin in the United States, write to Dept. DG, Penguin Books, 299 Murray Hill Parkway, East Rutherford, New Jersey 07073.

BY A WOMAN WRITT
Literature from Six Centuries by and about Women

Edited by Joan Goulianos

This is a unique collection of writings by and about women of six different centuries. "When women wrote," says Joan Goulianos, "they touched upon experiences rarely touched upon by men, they spoke in different ways about these experiences, they often wrote in different forms." Margery Kempe, a fourteenth-century wife and mother, described her struggles as a religious mystic. Aphra Behn, a seventeenth-century author and spy, wrote about passion. Mary Shelley, in the nineteenth century, evoked the loneliness of widowhood. Anaïs Nin, in the twentieth, plumbed the confusions and pleasures of the modern woman. It is to talented and courageous writers like these that we owe the works in *by a Woman writt,* works "in which women wrote about their lives and from which women and men today can draw insight about theirs." "Joan Goulianos's Introduction is superb. She asks all the right questions . . . an important book"—Erica Jong. "Brilliantly edited . . . the most exciting book of women's writings around"—Linda Wolfe. "Basic reading . . . in women's studies"—*Publishers Weekly.*

THE FIRST SEX

Elizabeth Gould Davis

Are women superior to men? This unique book aims to give woman her rightful place in history while repudiating what the author calls "2,000 years of propaganda." Drawing on science, mythology, archaeology, and history, Elizabeth Gould Davis comes up with some eye-opening facts: Biologically man is a mutant of woman, the Y chromosome a stunted X. . . . Ancient civilizations such as the Sumerian were matriarchal societies where women ruled and men were servants. . . . The collapse of these matriarchal societies signaled the brutalization of humanity and the increasing suppression of woman. . . . Woman was first in the discovery of the arts and sciences, first in the march toward civilization, and still first, according to biologists, in physical efficiency. That women are "the first sex" is, in fact, this book's inescapable conclusion. As the Introduction puts it, "The time has come to put woman back into the history books . . . to readmit her to the human race. Her contribution to civilization has been greater than man's, and man has overlooked her long enough." "The present intolerable world situation . . . cannot even begin to ease until the basic argument of Elizabeth Gould Davis's *The First Sex* is accepted by all schools and universities"—Robert Graves.

THE FUTURE OF MOTHERHOOD

Jessie Bernard

This provocative book is not *against* motherhood—it is *for* women . . .
and men. Declaring that motherhood as practiced in the United States
is harmful to both mothers and children, Dr. Jessie Bernard points out
that current attitudes toward maternity were determined in Victorian
England. As society begins to accept innovations like salaries for
housewives and even male hormone injections for noncompetitive
women, Dr. Bernard asks that each of the sexes share its particular
strengths with the other. Motherhood, she says, is too important to be
left to women alone—"and we are all in this together." "The first bal-
anced, historically and scientifically documented, and also predictive
view of women functioning in their most obvious role, the role of
mother"—*The New Republic.*

PSYCHOANALYSIS AND WOMEN

Edited by Jean Baker Miller, M.D.

These essays by sixteen eminent psychoanalysts revise Sigmund Freud's long-standing, phallocentric view of women. Karen Horney, Alfred Adler, Clara Thompson, Gregory Zilboorg, Mary Jane Sherfey, and others achieve a more realistic picture of the human female as they dispel myths about dependency, biological determinism, penis envy, and masochism. Their writings go on to explore the maternal instinct, childbearing, gender identity, and sexual identity and to comment on the role of women in literature. The result is a book that throws new light on psychoanalysis for women today and on women's continuing struggle for a more fulfilling way of life.

SEVEN WOMEN
Portraits from the American Radical Tradition

Judith Nies

Sarah Moore Grimké gave up her birthright as a Southern aristocrat and slaveholder to promote women's rights and abolition. Harriet Tubman, an escaped slave, led over three hundred other slaves to freedom on the Underground Railroad. Elizabeth Cady Stanton, who advocated women's rights to divorce, to property, and to the vote, was the first woman to run for Congress. Mother Jones, "the Joan of Arc of the coal fields," became one of the greatest spirits the American labor movement has ever seen. Charlotte Perkins Gilman called for the reform of America's two most cherished institutions: the home and motherhood. Anna Louise Strong, the journalist to whom Mao Tsetung granted his famous "paper tiger" interview, covered revolution in China and Russia. Dorothy Day, co-founder of the *Catholic Worker*, has fed and sheltered the hungry and homeless on New York City's Bowery for more than forty years. . . . A minority within a minority, these seven women stand out in a long tradition of American radicals who saw the madness of oppressive institutions. Sustained by a rare courage, they brought about far-reaching changes, sure that they would one day be seen as "messengers to the future." "Buy Nies's book and read it aloud faithfully, until all of you, young and old, have shared and incorporated into your vision of America the heroic, unique, and visionary contribution women have made to the history of these United States"—*Los Angeles Times*. "Inspiring reading for sympathetic readers of all ages"—*Publishers Weekly*.

VINDICATION OF THE RIGHTS OF WOMAN

Mary Wollstonecraft
Edited by Miriam Kramnick

Vindication of the Rights of Woman was published in 1792 and was received with a mixture of outrage and enthusiasm. In an age of ferment, following the American and French revolutions, Mary Wollstonecraft took prevailing egalitarian principles and dared to apply them to women. Her book is both a sustained argument for emancipation and an attack on a social and economic system. As Miriam Kramnick points out in her Introduction, subsequent feminists tended to lose sight of Wollstonecraft's radical objectives. For Mary Wollstonecraft all aspects of women's existence were interrelated, and any effective reform depended on a redistribution of political and economic power. Horace Walpole once called her "a hyena in petticoats," but it is a tribute to her forceful insight that modern feminists are finally returning to the arguments so passionately expressed in this remarkable book.

WOMAN'S BODY, WOMAN'S RIGHT
Birth Control in America

Linda Gordon

The history of birth control, which extends over thousands of years, has followed a devious, often underground, path in the United States. Widely practiced in ancient civilizations, most contraceptive methods, as well as abortion, were outlawed in America by 1850, but in the late nineteenth century American women began militating for the right to prevent or terminate pregnancy—and their long struggle led at last to gradual legalization. Tracing the story of the controversy through Theodore Roosevelt's attack on "race suicide," Margaret Sanger's pioneering crusade, the opposition of religious groups and male supremacists, and the flowering of today's women's movement, Linda Gordon shows that birth control has always been a matter of social and political acceptability rather than of medicine and technology. Indeed, until twenty years ago, modern medicine had contributed almost nothing to the improvement of devices "that were literally more than a millennium old." It was women, not doctors or scientists, who invented birth control—and it is today's women who must continue to assert their right to it. "A major contribution to the history that feminists *must* know if we are not to repeat it"—Adrienne Rich. "An impressive and well-documented piece of work, covering a number of sex-related issues not generally brought together in one place"—Mary S. Calderone, M.D. "Unusually important . . . daring and yet subtle in its interpretations, the book will become a focal point for future research and debate"—Martin Duberman.

WOMAN'S CONSCIOUSNESS, MAN'S WORLD

Sheila Rowbotham

"It seems to me that the cultural and economic liberation of women is inseparable from the creation of a society in which all people no longer have their lives stolen from them, and in which the conditions of their production and reproduction will no longer be distorted or held back by the subordination of sex, race, or class." Here Sheila Rowbotham, author of *Women, Resistance and Revolution,* adds her voice to the cause of women's liberation. In Part One she examines the development of the new feminist consciousness and describes the social changes that have triggered its growth. In Part Two she focuses her attention on women within the capitalist state and discusses the part they play in maintaining commodity production—showing how the family and sexuality at once reflect and influence other aspects of social and economic life. *Woman's Consciousness, Man's World* is both a valuable addition to the continuing debate about women in the twentieth century and an acute study of the structure of our society.

WOMEN AND CHILD CARE IN CHINA
A Firsthand Report

Ruth Sidel
Photographs by Victor W. Sidel

This firsthand report on the radically changing attitudes toward women and child rearing in today's China has dramatic implications for our own society. Ruth Sidel and her husband went to China as guests of the Chinese Medical Association. The book that resulted from their visit focuses on the amazingly rapid liberation of Chinese women from the "bitter past," when prostitution and venereal disease were rampant, marriages were made at an early age, and wives were virtually enslaved to their mothers-in-law. Now, Ms. Sidel reports, Chinese women are encouraged to take an active part in the life of the nation—and to help them do so, vast programs are providing birth-control information, prenatal assistance, maternity leaves, and childcare facilities. Most especially, *Women and Child Care in China* looks at nurseries, nursery schools, and kindergartens and at the revolutionary methods they employ. Ms. Sidel also compares Chinese childrearing practices with those in Israel and the Soviet Union, and she goes on to ask what aspects of the Chinese experience might be of value in the United States. "If you believe that a society can be significantly evaluated by the way its women and children live, you will find Ruth Sidel's *Women and Child Care in China* to be a useful and important addition to the literature about life today on the mainland"— CBS Radio.